To Be Honest

Championing Academic Integrity in Community Colleges

D1240893

WITHDRAWN

To Be Honest

Championing Academic Integrity in Community Colleges

Karén Clos Bleeker

Community College Press®

A division of the American Association of Community Colleges

Washington, DC

The American Association of Community Colleges (AACC) is the primary advocacy organization for the nation's community colleges. The association represents more than 1,200 two-year, associate degree–granting institutions and more than 11 million students. AACC promotes community colleges through five strategic action areas: recognition and advocacy for community colleges; student access, learning, and success; community college leadership development; economic and workforce development; and global and intercultural education. Information about AACC and community colleges may be found at www.aacc.nche.edu.

Design: Grace Design, LLC
Editor: Deanna D'Errico
Printer: Kirby Lithographic

© 2008 American Association of Community Colleges

Community College Press
American Association of Community Colleges
One Dupont Circle, NW
Suite 410
Washington, DC 20036

Printed in the United States of America.

Library of Congress Cataloging-in-Publication Data

Bleeker, Karen Clos.
    To be honest: championing academic integrity in community colleges/Karen Clos Bleeker.
       p. cm.
    "Defines academic dishonesty, summarizes research to date on its occurrence and prevalence in higher education, and offers recommendations to community colleges"—Provided by publisher.
    Includes bibliographical references.
    ISBN 978-0-87117-380-5
    1. Cheating (Education) 2. Community colleges—Corrupt practices. I. Title.

LB3609.B614 2007
378.1'958—dc22
                                                                                2007010018

Dedication

This book is dedicated to the memory of Dr. William Moore,
A. M. Aiken Regents Chair, and Professor,
Community College Leadership Program, of the University of Texas at Austin,
whose unapologetic devotion to ethics in higher education administration
remains forever in the hearts and minds of so many.

Contents

Foreword

This compelling book addresses a sensitive topic in an engaging manner. Hats off to Karén Clos Bleeker for articulating the problem of academic dishonesty in explicit terms and offering responses to the challenges that it poses, from the simplest, most naïve and uninformed acts of plagiarism to the most blatant and insensitive thefts of intellectual property.

As professionals and academics, we understand well the scope, the severity, and consequences of the crimes included under the umbrella term *academic dishonesty*. Professionals in our educational communities have been terminated for violating the rules and the sanctity of ethical principles. Whether the story is about a professor at a major university who was dismissed for submitting the work of others as his own or is about fabricated degrees or experience listed on a resume, the story has become familiar and no longer shocking.

We often address what is arguably the most basic act of academic dishonesty—plagiarism—as a sin of omission, not commission. In fact, it is safe to say that acts of plagiarism fall somewhere along an ethical continuum, from the uninformed and unintentional to the informed and intentional. The severity of the crime as we assess it must be tempered by a larger context in which we must consider the status of the culprit and then begin methodically to "inspect what we expect," that is, describe our expectations, how they are to be met, and the consequences of failure to meet them. Clearly, the responsibility for describing the context in which students have placed themselves is ours.

Years ago, an English teacher colleague described her shock at reading an "original" poem submitted by a student for a class assignment. It was well written, for sure, and Alfred Lord Tennyson probably thought so, too. The student chose to pass off "Crossing the Bar" as his own. Today, it is likely that a lesser-known verse might have gone undetected as being lifted. Ultimately, however, unlike cattle rustling in Texas, not all crimes of plagiarism are hanging offenses. They should be approached with responses appropriate to their criminal levels, preceded by rules and instruction that offer the same illustrations and warnings that are used in other civil and criminal venues.

Our parents taught us that the quality of one's character is most obvious when one's behavior is honestly and ethically predictable, whether we are behaving in private or the world is watching. The inner compass, that ethical steering mechanism that determines one's path, was a subject of conversation in our families. We were taught that our word was our bond and that our good name was our most precious possession. We wonder if current news and world reports are signaling that remarkably different conversations are being held in families, among friends and colleagues, and in corporate boardrooms.

More than 20 years ago, every student at St. Petersburg College in Florida was required to take an ethics course during his or her program of study. Today, we know of others in community colleges across the country, but requirements and courses vary widely. At The University of Texas at Austin, ethics courses abound. For the last 30 years, every student enrolled in our Community College Leadership Program has been required to complete a full-semester course on ethics in theory and practice.

A most compelling two-part question comes to mind. What did students bring with them to this study, and what will (should) they take away? It is clear that these students will be entering a quite different world than we entered as young professionals and academics. Not for the faint-hearted, the journey upon which they will embark in the not-so-distant future will challenge their core values and the strength of their convictions. But on the whole, while singular courses make an important statement about an institution's commitment to addressing this compelling topic, undergraduate and graduate students alike are better served when ethics, honesty, and integrity are taught, developed, and practiced throughout the curriculum and the institution.

This timely book was written with a strong commitment to sounding the call to arms about a growing and deceptively benign challenge to our somewhat naïve perception that an honest conduct of affairs has been the order of the day. It presents evidence that things are not always as they seem. As Clos Bleeker began writing this book, she described some current events that illustrated the premise of the book. As she completed her work, the events of the day were offering even greater testimony of the challenges we face, as we are now awash in news of dishonest, unethical, and treacherous behavior at the highest public and private levels.

We appreciate and applaud Clos Bleeker's critical approach to a problem that will not go away, that stands to eat away at our core values of decency and honor, and that must be addressed in uncompromising fashion at every level of educational institutions. Although you will find little joy in this book, you will find hope and be better armed to take action after digesting its contents.

Suanne D. and John E. Roueche
The University of Texas at Austin

Acknowledgments

Nothing makes authors shudder like the prospect of thanking those who made significant contributions to their books. Perhaps that is why so few of the books on my library shelf actually have acknowledgment sections for me to borrow from.

Never mind. I suppose that isn't as funny as I'd hoped it would be. I know this is a book on academic integrity. I know I couldn't—even if I were so inclined—possibly copy someone else's acknowledgment section. But I am worried. What if I fail to remember someone? I'm of an age where that is as likely to happen as it isn't and, well, I don't mind when it's just me, searching for my sunglasses for the umpteenth time that day when an observant 2-year-old could have told me that they are pushed up on my head like an oversized headband. But forgetting someone I owe a debt of gratitude to? Well, that's different. So I am approaching the acknowledgment section with a great deal of caution. If you do not see yourself mentioned here, do not assume I am an ingrate. Addle-headed, yes. Ungrateful, no.

Let's begin at the beginning. There are a few people who have made such significant contributions that this book simply would not have been possible without them. My editor is first on that list. Left to my own devices, I'd have turned this book into something the size of the New York City phone book. Deanna D'Errico would have none of that. Thank you for keeping me from getting tangled up in my own prose.

To Drs. John and Suanne Roueche, good friends and mentors, who, when asked, graciously agreed to offer an introduction for this text. As a former student of both and an ardent admirer of their work, I am honored that, in this endeavor, we are bound by the same book covers.

To Dr. Don McCabe, founding president of the Center for Academic Integrity and gentleman scholar who made research available to me for inclusion in this book, who gave of his time to read drafts of chapters and offer suggestions, and whose tireless devotion to the topic of academic dishonesty has provided much-needed illumination of a vexing and persistent issue.

To the faculty, staff, administration, and board members of Temple College who have allowed to me to work among them for the past 4 years. I hope I tell you often enough how much I value serving among you, how much I respect the goodness of your minds and hearts, your steadfast student orientation, and your dedication to integrity. And to the library staff, who never tired of my obscure requests for information, especially Todd Hively and Kathy Fulton. As I have said before, "You guys rock!"

And last, but not least, to Harry. Who loves me more than I deserve and who thinks I am smarter and braver than I actually am.

Introduction

I never thought of myself as an expert on the subject of academic dishonesty. I am not in league with those, many of whom are highlighted in the forthcoming chapters, who have conducted extensive research studies or tested complex hypotheses about students who cheat and why. My knowledge of academic dishonesty is rooted in the humble soil of fate and experience. Years ago, I was the chief academic officer of a rural community college in the Midwest. I was well prepared for the traditional ethical predicaments, not so prepared to confront academic dishonesty from an organizational or cultural perspective. This situation would have to be "suited up for" and without much notice or forewarning. As anyone functioning in a leadership capacity may tell you, the predictable challenges are comparatively easy to handle. They are the things you can see coming. With these, there is opportunity to plan, to solicit input, to deliberate, and, with any luck at all, to eventually overcome. But it is those events that take you by surprise on a random Wednesday afternoon, the issues that come from nowhere and refuse to be put down, that are fraught with the most peril.

My experience with academic dishonesty began simply enough and is chronicled in an article titled "When Academic Dishonesty Happens on Your Campus," excerpted here as follows:

> Last year, our college experienced a rash of cheating incidents that caused us to re-evaluate how prepared we were to deal with academic dishonesty. Within two weeks after a seemingly isolated incident in which one of our professors discovered a student cheating on a written assignment, four separate incidents of academic dishonesty were reported in our on-line program, in outreach and community education, and on-campus programs, as well. What had happened? In no particular order, the incidents included one student copying answers from another during a biology final; three students turning in essays downloaded from an Internet term-paper site and the teacher re-evaluating their essays and, thus, their grades; a teacher mistakenly handing out

a draft copy of the final exam while distributing graded quizzes and, upon realizing the error, giving the unwitting recipient the opportunity to return it without assumption of dishonesty (no one stepped forward, and he had to revise the original); and, two otherwise average students gaining entry to a teacher's office in an unguarded moment, spotting a folder containing the final exam for their algebra course, liberating it, and caught studying it in the library the next morning. Needless to say, the expressions of alarm and disdain echoed across the campus: "What's happening?" "What can we do?" "How could this have been prevented?" But not all of the complications could be blamed on dishonesty. Some of the problems stemmed from our own neglect. We had been operating on an outdated and semi-relevant policy that clearly affected the punishment that could be meted out. However, in our defense, it is easy to see how it happened. It may have been that some of us would have preferred to remain unfamiliar with the ugly and inevitable truth. Some students will cheat! So there we were: a college within a community where folks seldom lock their doors at night, where sleep is undisturbed by the prospect of crime or criminals, where they look after one another's children with a casual neighborliness that could only be the result of many generations experiencing hardship, and where a handshake is an acceptable expression of honesty. Yet, the unthinkable had happened here, and so we asked: *What is to be done when a college finds itself confronted with dishonest behavior?* And then we focused on seeking answers and taking action. (Clos, 2002, p. 1)

In the next year and a half, we consulted the Center for Academic Integrity (CAI), established an Academic Integrity Task Force, invited faculty and staff participation, and conducted an integrity audit. Using a CAI instrument, we surveyed more than 763 students and 119 full- and part-time faculty members, asking students to self-report cheating behavior and asked faculty to report their perceptions of the issue. The results were startling, but among the most notable was one irrefutable truth: A significant percentage of the students admitted cheating, saw no harm in it, and acknowledged no act of academic dishonesty as "serious."

Perhaps surprisingly, the data also revealed that a significant number of students were aware of academic dishonesty and fervently wanted it to stop. These students supported the revision of college policy in percentages higher than those reported by faculty (and those were pretty high), even when that meant establishing the *XF* grade. As a result of the integrity audit, the survey results were shared in an open forum, and a policy was crafted that addressed the issue of academic dishonesty from a new angle, one that a neighboring university had found success with. Academic dishonesty would be identified as an academic disciplinary matter, and faculty would be able to recommend sanctions for violations of the college's academic integrity policy, ranging from issuing verbal warnings to recommending the *XF* grade.

During the next year or so, incidents of academic dishonesty were adjudicated by individual faculty members, some of whom recommended the *XF* grade and some of whom did not. But the differentiation in sanctions did not really matter. What did matter was that there was finally a sense of empowerment, a feeling that we had done something purposeful to address academic dishonesty. There was not total consensus, but the problem had been recognized and met with an appropriate and thoughtful policy response.

Maybe no one, with the possible exception of me, actually thought that the work that had been done would put an end to academic dishonesty, but it was nice to reflect on what had been done and what might be prevented. At least, that is, until the day representatives from the National Collegiate Athletic Association (NCAA) and a neighboring university arrived in the president's office, asking questions about courses and grades that had been received by three former student athletes. When asked, I assisted NCAA in its investigation and, under the supervision of the president, conducted a campus-based examination of the academic irregularities that had occurred. In the beginning, I had no sense of perspective. How could I? Nothing like this had ever happened at any other college in which I had worked. What I knew about such things I knew from what I had read in the *Chronicle of Higher Education* or seen on television. No one could have known at that point how long the investigation would go on, how much would be discovered, or how deep the quicksand of controversy would become.

At first, I worked on the investigation sporadically, responding to questions posed by NCAA officials and at least one of the 4-year universities. I did what many administrators would have done. I kept the file on my desk for only as long as necessary to bring closure to whatever the recent concerns were. Then I would sigh and put it away and return to any one of the dozens of things that needed my attention that day. It was not until I had collected enough documentation to break the rubber band around the manila folder that held everything, reluctantly transferring the information to a 2-inch three-ring notebook, that I realized that the investigation might not end any time soon, as I had originally hoped and expected.

Before too long, the documentation had become like miles of perverse knitting that, once removed from the needles, just kept unraveling into one unsavory pile after another. By the time I had enough documentation to fill a fourth 3-inch notebook, I could not deny the sense of rage and disbelief that had begun to follow me around like a persistent depressing shadow. Just as had been done when the college first confronted the episodic but isolated acts of cheating that had occurred earlier, I again began to question everything I had known or thought I had known about academic dishonesty. So much had been done (or so I thought) to emphasize and protect a culture that valued academic integrity, yet in the face of what was unfolding before me, it seemed to have been all been for naught. Ironically, unlike with the first experience, the college had better prepared, but despite those best efforts, little had actually changed. We had underestimated the enemy.

Among other things, the results of the multiple investigations pointed to a series of offenses, ranging from academic dishonesty to mail fraud to financial aid fraud. Offenses included the purposeful falsification of work-study hours for student athletes; misrepresentation of GED credentials; creation of sham PE classes, which either never met or reflected an extraordinary lack of rigor; and the registration of student athletes in a variety of "correspondence school" and distance education courses that effectively awarded credit for work they may not have done themselves and grades they almost certainly had not earned. Even the college's own online courses had not been untouched by those seeking an end around. Such offenses were not limited to basketball players, although that group certainly represented the lion's share of abuse. Before it was over, I had heard from a student who had been on the college's cheerleading team who had allegedly been told by the coach and her spouse that she should enroll for a class that she would never be expected to attend but would receive credit for. The student confided in a friend, who advised her to go to the assistant coach, who came to me. By the time I spoke to them, the student was, quite honorably, asking to have the ill-gotten credit removed from her transcript. A request which, to this day, stands out in my mind like a bright spot on an otherwise ominous horizon.

The scheme, it seems, was designed for the sole purpose of awarding academic credit to athletes in need of academic rehabilitation for the sake of eligibility at Division I universities. Those who were closest to the story that would eventually come to national attention have speculated that some "juco" coaches engage in such behavior in an attempt to move on and up by ingratiating themselves to coaches who are in a position to help further their careers. The students, it seems, and the futures they lay to waste with such behavior, are incidental to the overriding desire for career advancement.

In a *Sports Illustrated* article titled "The Dark Side," the college's former athletic director, Neil Elliott, admitted, "It was clear to me that Ryan [men's head basketball coach] was doing everything he could to land a job at a Division I school. That was his focus above everything else" (Dohrmann, 2005). This speculation was confirmed in the same article by Dan Sparks, president of the NJCAA Coaches Association, whose comments reflected on the mindset of "many juco coaches." He observed, "We have a lot of them, mostly young coaches, who get tied up with assistants at four-year school…. They think that if they do the [4-year coaches'] dirty work for them, it will land them a Division I job" (Dohrmann, 2005). Dave "Soupy" Campbell (then the college's basketball coach) summed up the pitiful reality, adding, "The truth is, the four-year guys prostitute the junior college coaches…. That's not a good word to use, but that is what is going on" (Dohrmann, 2005).

In the end, what I (and a few others) came to know beyond all reasonable doubt was that at least three former student athletes (and, in all likelihood, more) had received hundreds of hours of unearned academic credit for courses. I knew that degrees had been granted that were the result of intentional acts of academic fraud and misrepresentation and that they had been innocently endorsed by the college's leadership, myself included. I knew that the scheme had been deliberately perpetrated over a relatively long period of time by people who held positions of trust. When the results of the investigation were as complete as they could be, I submitted, through the president to the board, recommendations for addressing what had been found. When prevented from effecting a just course of action, I offered my resignation. My own sense of integrity prevented me from going any further.

As fate would have it, I was to receive an offer of employment from Temple College, and, sitting across the table from the man who was to become my new boss, I conveyed all that had happened. Not as therapy, mind you, but because I knew only too well that what had happened was very likely to play out on a national stage and I did not want him to make an offer to a vice presidential candidate without knowing about the baggage that could show up on his doorstep. As a man of integrity himself, he did not flinch. He offered his support, his condolences, and his full confidence. I am remiss in never having told him that, in that one moment, he restored to me all of the faith I thought I had lost in others. He is too humble to hear it from me, but he is my hero.

It is from the context of these events (now almost half a decade in the past) that this book was conceived—partly out of anger, partly out of sorrow, partly out of a sense of regret and unrealized reckoning, and partly out of a longing to do something, anything, to keep this from happening to other community colleges and to other people who have not earned the humiliation of scandal. What weighs most heavily on me is the memory of what happens to the people in a college when something like this happens. Good people worked at the college where this happened. Good people whose only misfortune was to have been there at the wrong point in the college's history. When the headlines in the local newspaper decry multiple indictments, federal financial aid fraud, and purposeful deceit and academic fraud, it is the good people who suffer before justice is meted out to those who truly deserve punishment.

As I said in the beginning of this introduction, I am not an expert. I have not conducted large-scale research studies, nor have I been recognized for my insights or innovative approaches to this issue—at least not yet. But, like so many of you, I have stood face to face with this enemy and was not vanquished. I have been bloodied and bruised by it, as have good people for whom I cared deeply, but we survived it. I hope that the tragedy I have described—and tragedy is not too strong a word—and the contents of this book will help us all, individually and collectively, summon the strength to purposefully identify, confront, and eliminate academic dishonesty as it occurs within community colleges.

CHAPTER ONE

Academic Dishonesty and the Community College: Putting the Problem in Perspective

Introduction

If research findings are to be believed, you can be more than fairly certain that academic dishonesty can be found somewhere on your campus, perhaps in your courses, at this very moment. If you are an administrator, odds are good that at least some of the grades awarded by your faculty in good faith and applied conscientiously toward the graduation requirements of your college's degrees are tainted by those who may have made a less than noble academic effort. Likewise, it is no exaggeration to assume that the academic efforts of those students making an honest effort are adversely affected by those who cheat and remain undetected or, worse, unchallenged. If this sounds improbable, consider the following basic statistics:

- There are approximately 1,200 community colleges in the United States.
- More than 11 million students are enrolled in community colleges.
- Hundreds of millions of credit hours are being earned by community college students in a wide array of liberal arts, developmental, and career–technical courses.
- Researchers estimate that a minimum of 40% and a maximum of 80% of students asked to self-report cheating behavior admitted to at least one act of cheating.

If the laws of probability are reliable, those facts alone are convincing evidence that academic dishonesty is alive on community college campuses.

The fact that the research has, for the most part, not yielded a single, common, or widely applied definition of academic dishonesty does little to help abate the occurrence of it. Furthermore, not only do faculty, staff, and administrators fail to agree on a single definition, but also perceptions of what behaviors constitute academic dishonesty differ. Dalton (1998, p. 5) defined academic dishonesty as "a wide variety of behaviors that are regarded as unethical," and he confirmed that, for students, the definitions of right and wrong, as it pertained to academic dishonesty, were even less defined than for the faculty. "Their definitions for what constitutes cheating," he observed, "are less rigorous than those of faculty and more open to situational factors. Even faculty disagree about standards that define cheating and thus may send mixed or confusing messages to students" (pp. 5–6). The question of what does—or does not—constitute academic dishonesty (and to whom) has us drawing subjective and differing lines in the air to navigate the uncertain territory between opinion and behavior.

The Societal Context

Dishonesty is not an unfamiliar cultural issue. In fact, it can be easily argued that every generation has expressed the belief that it teetered upon the precipice of an impending moral decline. In a brilliantly chronicled look at dishonesty, *The Cheating Culture: Why More Americans Are Doing Wrong to Get Ahead*, Callahan confirmed that evidence of cheating is all around us, influencing not only the decisions made by students in an education context, but also our behavior in other aspects of our lives.

> Cheating is everywhere. By cheating, I mean breaking the rules to get ahead academically, professionally, or financially. Some of this cheating involves violating the law; some does not. Either way, most of it is by people who, on the whole, view themselves as upstanding members of society. Again and again, Americans who wouldn't so much as shoplift a pack of chewing gum are committing felonies at tax time, betraying the trust of their patients, misleading investors, ripping off their insurance company, or lying to their clients.
>
> Something strange is going on here. Americans seem to be using two moral compasses. One directs our behavior when it comes to things like sex, family, drugs, and traditional forms of crime. A second provides us ethical guidance in the realm of career, money, and success. The obvious question is: Where did we pick up that second compass? (Callahan, 2004, p. 15)

Callahan offered four key reasons that dishonest behavior seems to have gained such momentum: new pressures to succeed in an increasingly competitive social, economic, and vocational environment; bigger rewards for winning; increased temptation and weaker safeguards against wrongdoing; and trickle-down corruption described as the perception that "everyone else is doing it" (2004, pp. 20–23). Whereas it might be easy to dismiss the theory that more people are finding it easier to rationalize away a diminished ability to recognize right from wrong, it might be decidedly more difficult to convince a nation of educators that academic dishonesty—specifically, cheating—is not becoming worse. Dishonesty is remarkably persistent, traversing the evolution of higher education in one form or another, only to have found new life with the introduction of new technologies and a culture increasingly unfamiliar with or indifferent to the value of values.

Other social observers have been troubled by the apparent lack of integrity that has burrowed its way into our culture. Carter (1996) asked us to reflect upon the events of the past decade and to consider our diminishing familiarity with morality with "just a handful of examples":

> Drawn from the headlines of the mid-1990s, the winner of the Miss Virginia pageant is stripped of her title after officials determine that her educational credentials are false; a television network is forced to apologize for using explosives to add a bit of verisimilitude to a tape purporting to show that a particular truck is unsafe; and the authors of a popular book on management are accused of using bulk purchases at key stores to manipulate the *New York Times* best-seller list. Go back a few more years and we can add in everything from a slew of Wall Street titans imprisoned for violating a bewildering variety of laws in their frantic effort to get ahead, to the women's Boston marathon winner branded a cheater for spending part of the race on the subway. But cheating is evidently no big deal: some 70 percent of college students admit to having done it at least once. (p. 4)

The Higher Education Context

As Carter (1996) suggested, there seems to be no shortage of disturbing social, political, legal, economic, religious, and educational events that would lead us to believe that dishonesty persists even in those organizations that have had, at least ostensibly, a deeply rooted moral foundation. Community colleges are no exception. Faculty members within those institutions have good reason to find academic dishonesty particularly offensive; so do honest community college students. But unlike those whose careers are made in politics, business, or entertainment where such things have, unfortunately, become increasingly common, many of those who have spent years legitimately pursuing and passing on knowledge find dishonesty a particularly detestable enemy.

First, they realize that the foundation of their careers, regardless of discipline, rests upon the honest pursuit of knowledge. Additionally, they know that the degrees they have earned are not the means to a different end or a commodity to be exchanged, but rather are evidence of a lifelong commitment to learning. Furthermore, those who dedicate their careers and lives to teaching and learning acknowledge that their careers rest upon a foundation of honesty. Without that foundation, learning is reduced to a hollow and rhetorical exercise, devoid of any real value. Even if we seldom discuss it or give it the thoughtful attention that it deserves, we know that education without integrity is like religion without faith.

Those of us who make our careers in higher education today do not do so from within the ivory towers of our predecessors, nor do we enjoy the benefit of the doubt extended by the constituencies of a previous era. As a result, the reputation they enjoyed—deserved or not—provides significantly less shelter than that of generations past. Increasingly, governing bodies, accrediting agencies, state legislatures, and society in general demand greater accountability from educators—perhaps with good reason.

One need only to look back less than two and a half decades to find strong evidence of a tax-paying citizenry growing less convinced of the efficacy of higher education and more vocal in its support of significant change. And although it must be said that the dissatisfaction results, at least in part, from two factors critical to higher education—public funding and accountability—we may do well to consider the often complicated nature of this debate and the potential impact that might result were the same citizenry (and their respective elected officials) to become similarly disenchanted with or curious about the extent to which we actively protect the integrity of our courses, the sanctity of the grades received, and the degrees that are the cumulative effect of both.

It is within this uncomfortable context that higher education in general —and community colleges in particular—find themselves facing yet another challenge, one perhaps that they have yet to fully acknowledge: the threat presented by ever-increasing levels of academically dishonest behavior among students. Should anyone doubt the imperative presented by this most recent development, we need only remind ourselves of the all too familiar outcry that accompanies public revelations of dishonesty as it occurs within education.

Recall, for example, an incident in Piper, Kansas, in the spring of 2002, in which a high school teacher, Christine Pelton, discovered that a majority of students in her biology class had plagiarized their assigned papers. She did what any of us would deem reasonable: She consulted institutional policy and awarded a failing grade to 28 sophomores. Ultimately, however, she was directed by the school board to lessen the punishment when the parents of the students complained. She resigned the next day amid much media attention and the dismay of a community stunned by such a public demonstration of board interference and misplaced values. Michael Josephson, founder and president of the Josephson Institute of Ethics, acknowledged that "this kind of thing is happening every day around the country, where people with integrity are not being backed by their organization" (Josephson Institute of Ethics, 2002).

If it seems easy to dismiss the misfortune of a single high school teacher based on the presumption that lapses of integrity are more common occurrences in high schools, consider the misfortune experienced by Barton County Community College in rural Kansas. After a year-long investigation by college and federal officials, former basketball coach Ryan Wolf was accused of misdeeds including fabricating grades for classes that were either nonexistent or pitifully lacking in academic quality, committing bank fraud, and misappropriating federal financial aid funds. One author, writing for *Sports Illustrated*, suggested that Wolf placed his desire to obtain employment within a Division I university above his professional obligation to both his students and his former employer—and did what was necessary to achieve that goal (Dohrmann, 2005).

The Community College Context

The problem of academic dishonesty is further complicated by the fact that, although there may be much written on this topic, very little of the existing research focuses on the issue in the specific context of the community college. Because researchers have focused primarily on 4-year colleges and universities, we know with some certainty the details of how this issue affects those institutions. We know with some certainty that traditional undergraduate students seem to cheat with more frequency than ever before and that they appear to do so with less conscience. We know their strategies, rationale, and motivations.

We also know how academic dishonesty affects those who encounter it. We have chronicled the dismay and determination of any number of faculty members and administrators and can point to example after example of institutional responses designed to stem the rising tide of dishonesty and to protect the honest students who deserve a more level playing field. We are familiar with a variety of recommendations regarding policies and punishments, many of which have been implemented—with varying degrees of efficiency—in a number of colleges and universities across the country. We acknowledge that those precautionary measures have been designed to discourage people who do not share our commitment to integrity and, if possible, to provide an opportunity for rehabilitation.

What we do not know is the extent to which academic dishonesty is present in community colleges—whether they are more vulnerable, whether community college students cheat more or less, or whether their reasons for cheating are different from those of other students. We do not know how many of us have policies in place to address dishonesty when it occurs or if those policies have been at all effective. Additionally, we know very little about the organizational psychology of the problem. For example, are there differences in the perceptions of university and community college faculty? Are our administrators more—or less—prepared, knowledgeable, or committed? Can they ensure that any decision they might make with respect to this issue would be the kind of decision they would be glad to see revealed 6 inches above the fold of their local newspaper? Are they prepared to confront dishonesty when it occurs within their institutions, or are their time and energy spent elsewhere? Do our boards of trustees acknowledge the imminent threat presented by this issue? Do our accrediting agencies or the federal government expect us to demonstrate a commitment to academic integrity? And what do we know of our communities? Are we able to demonstrate to our constituencies that we acknowledge integrity as an essential element of not just what we do, but how we do it?

Perhaps the answers to these and many other as-yet unasked questions are found in a simple good news–bad news analysis. Compared with 4-year colleges and universities, community colleges are relatively new institutions, many having been brought into existence in the mid-1960s. That fact, combined with the profound differences in our respective missions—not to mention the "second-class citizenship" still experienced in some areas—would be enough to explain why so much research on this topic has focused on traditional 4-year colleges and universities. The good news, however, is that we may be able to draw quite a bit from the research of others, even if that research is based on a population of students not entirely like our own.

There have been, after all, a number of researchers who have addressed academic dishonesty (albeit from a variety of perspectives); without their work, it would most certainly be more difficult to address the problem in community colleges. A brief look back may provide another explanation: Some of the seminal work on the topic was just beginning as community colleges began to form and grow. Alschuler and Bliming (1995) provided a research retrospective beginning with the work of Bowers (1964), who, more than 40 years ago, contended that the problem has been underestimated by members of the campus community for at least 30 years. Citing the findings of several milestone studies, Alschuler and Bliming stated,

> If anything, the levels of cheating have increased since 1941 (Lundeman, 1988). In a national study of 6,096 students at 31 schools (McCabe, 1994), one-third of the students admitted copying from another student during a test, using crib notes, or helping someone else cheat. Up to half the students admitted plagiarizing, falsifying, or using dishonest methods of complete assignments. Two-thirds have seen others cheat, but protect their classmates with an informal code of silence. Ninety-five percent believe it is unlikely that students will report students. These data are consistent with results of other studies (Baird, 1980; Collison, 1990; Ethics of American Youth, 1990; Haines, Diekhoff, LaBeff, and Clark, 1986; Hetherington and Feldman, 1964; Janya, 1991; Jendrek, 1989; Michaels and Meithe, 1989; Wellborn, 1980; Zastrow, 1970). (1995, p. 123)

At this point, it is difficult to know the extent to which academic dishonesty is present in our community colleges. It is possible, however, to take stock of what others have found, to make a candid evaluation of our situational context, and to take action from there. What can we know? For starters, we know that cheating in an education context is not a new phenomenon. And if it is true that the best predictor of future behavior is past behavior, we can surmise that it is likely to continue happening. What has changed is our reaction to it, our innate ability to recognize—or perhaps defend—right from wrong.

There are those who would suggest that we live in such complicated times that old-fashioned notions of good and evil are inadequate concepts better suited to simpler times. We know that cheating, especially the kind that occurs in an educational environment, is occurring more often and with younger children. Some researchers believe it begins as early as the first or second grade. Huber (2004) found that for some students, cheating becomes a part of life during the first academic year in which grades are assigned. She quoted one third grade teacher who said, "It really starts when you're learning content. When you're learning letters, you can't really cheat" (p. 23).

We know that there is increased pressure on students to perform academically in order to secure a successful future. For better or worse, children realize at younger ages the value of things and what it takes to keep them. Bushweller (1999) chronicled the persistence of cheating not just in high schools, but in elementary and middle schools as well. He cited an example of a teacher who gave two second-grade classes and two fifth-grade classes spelling words to study and told them they would be tested on the words the next day. In half the classes, she offered candy bars to anyone getting all the words right. She graded the papers but did not mark them. When she asked the students to grade their own papers and compared the students' grades with hers, she found that among the students who were not offered candy bars, only one student cheated by changing wrong answers to correct ones. In the other two classes, all but three students cheated just to get the candy bar. Bushweller (1999) also offered an explanation for why cheating occurs:

> Many educators say the rise in cheating is due to an erosion of ethics in a self-centered culture. Some point to habits ingrained in students through years of working together in cooperative learning situations. Others pin the blame on teachers who don't care if kids cheat or who would rather avoid the hassle of disciplining those who do. Still others bemoan growing numbers of indulgent parents who refuse to hold their kids accountable.... The real cause of the cheating epidemic is all of the above, says Michael Josephson, president of the Josephson Institute of Ethics. What's more, he says there has been a shifting of worries. "In recent years, people are so much more concerned about drugs and violence. Cheating is getting worse, but it's getting less attention." (p. 25)

The Impact of Technology

Perhaps no other single occurrence of our generation—with the possible exception of desegregation—has had the unparalleled effect on education that the introduction of new technology has. What once took hours to do is now made simpler, faster, and cheaper because of the existence of a variety of new technologies. In the classroom, technology has allowed teachers and students alike to go places and do things that once seemed impossible. Today, in an era when computers are common and the Internet is essential, both teachers and students are changed dramatically by the existence of things that were unavailable only a decade ago. Computers, laptops, wireless access, digital cameras, advanced graphing calculators, the Internet, and millions of Web sites, as well as cell phones capable of recording, photographing, and text messaging, have permanently altered the way we do almost everything, including communicate, interact, work, play, educate, shop, and, yes, cheat.

Moeck (2002) provided a nostalgic look at the means of cheating: "In the 1960s, freshmen students heard stories about the sorority and fraternity house file cabinets bulging with treasure troves of academic goodies and filled with copies of completed examinations, term papers, laboratory practical examinations, and other types of academic paraphernalia" (p. 479). Today's "treasure troves" are more likely to be found by electronic means. In *Academic Dishonesty: An Educator's Guide*, Whitley and Keith-Spiegel (2002), citing Goldsmith (1998), noted that "modern technology—in the form of hand-held computers, programmable calculators, and so forth—has provided students with the ability to compile electronic crib notes" (p. 95).

Research findings by Donald McCabe, director of the Center for Academic Integrity (CAI), strongly indicate that plagiarism is on the rise in the nation's colleges and universities. He observed that "Internet plagiarism is a growing concern on all campuses as students struggle to understand what constitutes acceptable use of the Internet" (cited in Finkel, 2005, p. 7). Further on this point, he added,

> In the absence of clear direction from the faculty, most students have concluded that "cut and paste" plagiarism—using a sentence or two (or more) from different sources online and weaving this information together into a paper without appropriate citation—is not a serious issue. While 10 percent of students admitted to engaging in such behavior in 1999, this rose to 41

percent in a 2001 survey, with the majority of students (68 percent) suggesting this was not a serious issue. (cited in Finkel, 2005, p. 7)

Today, students at all levels of education are aware of the phenomenal ease with which they can ease their workloads by downloading any number of essays, term papers, assignments, and examinations. In a teaching effectiveness seminar titled "Cheating 101: Paper Mills and You," Fain and Bates (2005) noted that there were more than 250 active Internet term paper sites and 71 specific term paper sites whose sole purpose was to offer prewritten papers. One site— CheatHouse.com—lured new users by boasting that 1.5 million term papers were downloaded daily. One need apply only some basic math to realize that the odds of those purloined papers finding their way onto our own campuses are very high indeed. And, if you think such sites are only for those students with ready income access, think again. In answer to the question of how much it costs to get a paper, they found the following policies:

- No charge or no charge with a required registration.
- No charge, but you must submit a paper in exchange.
- A one-time membership fee that allows subsequent access.
- A per-page charge of $1–$10 per page, payable by credit card.
- Express delivery for an extra charge.
- Custom papers written for an exorbitant fee.
- Sales and summer blowout specials. (Fain & Bates, 2005)

Not to be left out of the profit to be generated by academic chicanery, other Internet-savvy entrepreneurs have seized upon yet another economic opportunity to tempt those looking for an academic shortcut. A foray onto eBay, searching only the words *term papers*, produced 45 results, with papers for sale from $.99 to $79.99. One item was listed as follows:

Do you have a 10 page paper due? Procrastination got you down? School life is hard enough without the extra stress. I can help you with that last minute essay and that last bit of research. This paper can be delivered in four days. It will be custom written to your specifications. What do you need to do? Email me and tell me what your essay/research is all about. Send me the information your professor gave you about the essay and what guidelines need to be followed. Pay through Paypal and within three days you will have your essay emailed to you. If you need a longer or shorter paper, check the other items in my store. The bibliography page or pages are free. I have written custom essays for years. Since September, I have written on average six a week. I have two degrees and lots of experience. (eBay item #5968796631, April 10, 2005)

Some of the more notable items listed included a lot of 17 original term papers ($79.99), a database of term papers and book reports for high school and college ($14.99), an essay/term paper Web site ($10.99), a 1947 thesis on ceramic engineering ($19.99), and a single CD with more than 6,545 "top-quality research papers" for only $4.95. Perhaps predictably, none of the item descriptions referenced the certain ethical or possible legal complications inherent to the electronic trafficking of academic goods and services. And while eBay does an exceptional job of protecting its community of buyers and sellers from the availability of unauthentic items such as faux Vuitton bags or Chanel sunglasses, it seems to have paid markedly less attention to the buying and selling of essays, term papers, and even dissertations to those with the inclination, technology, and financial wherewithal to take advantage. In short, not just on eBay, but on virtually all other sites like it, almost anything goes (for a price), including the integrity of the buyers and sellers of such items.

Replacing the word *essay* for the word *research paper* on eBay produced similar results, yielding 54 items, including legitimate books on how to write research papers and a variety of style manuals. Five items, however, offered research papers for sale. In one listing, the seller wrote, "Go to the website for tonnes [sic] of positive feedback and writing samples.... I employ only the best grad students and professors" (eBay item #5968256367, April 12, 2005).

Searching the term *college essay* produced only eight results, but one of the items, "A-Grade Quality College Essays/Term Papers $7 per Page," deserves special mention. The description began as follows:

Term Papers Keeping You Up Late? Can't define your thesis? Don't understand the importance of topic sentences? Lost trying to figure out how to properly cite journal articles using the APA and MLA styles? Struggling to find some last minute research articles, studies, and ideas to cite in your own term paper? I provide A-Grade term papers

- Custom written on your specific topic
- Completely non-plagiarized
- Written by experienced writers
- Delivered before your deadline (eBay item #5969174826, April 10, 2005)

The seller listed "distinct features" such as "personalized attention to your needs from a firm with a small, experienced staff"; "writers holding a Master's degrees [sic], along with writing experience of no less than 25 years"; Retired Teachers [sic], Faculty [sic], etc."; "the relief of having FREE Title Page, Bibliography and References, Research Work, Formatting/Stylization [sic]."

Referencing "custom papers" provided by a "staff of writers," the seller stated that products were "100% original" and "one of a kind," providing an alphabetical list of potential topics ranging from Africa and anatomy to women's issues and world affairs. Along with a list of stipulations including how orders should be submitted and that ample preparation time is needed, the seller emphasized the "handmade nature" of what was being sold, adding that "depending on the level of difficulty and the number of pages you require, we can conduct the necessary research, write the paper from scratch, and email it to you in as little as 1 week" (eBay item #5969426815, April 13, 2005).

What is most interesting, however, is this statement: "Can You Use it [sic] As Your Own Term Paper? Not even one sentence. Plagiarism occurs when you take the ideas OR words of another writer and restate them as your own without proper attribution to that writer as the original source. My work is designated to assist students in preparation of their own work" (eBay item #5969426815, April 13, 2005). However, with that said, the seller continued with another page and a half of specific descriptive information, designed for no other practical purpose than to sell a completed paper. "Just send us your term paper topic, specifications and deadline through eBay mail. The more precise your details are, the more convenient it would be for our writers to ascertain whether your request is feasible and, if accepted, these specifications will be used to create your term paper" (eBay item #5969426815, April 13, 2005).

And, of course, no deal is concluded until the financial details are precisely outlined and agreed upon. To that end, the seller offered a few words to clarify the price for a custom-written paper presumably designed only to assist students in the preparation of their own work:

> The $700 [sic] "buy it now option" pays for one page. I will send you an invoice requesting the additional funds of $7.00 per additional page. As soon as payment is received in full, our writers *immediately* start working on them *immediately* [sic] [emphasis added]. The topic is properly researched, relevant material collected, outline developed, and finally the compilation process of your term paper [sic]. From its conception to its compilation, to its final delivery, your term paper goes through our various departments such as the proofreading department, etc. (eBay item #5969426815, April 13, 2005)

Given the quality of the prose in the description, it may be safe to assume that the seller or "marketing department" (not the "proofreading department") was responsible for the many errors evident in the tortured (and sometimes fragmented) sentence structure, irregular capitalization, and repetition of identical words in the same phrase. What the seller failed to acknowledge is that English teachers are usually picky about such things, even when they see them in papers that are not designed to purposefully effect an academic fraud but are produced innocently and with proper ethical foresight.

A Call to Action

Almost every researcher who has examined the phenomenon of academic dishonesty has remarked on its persistent nature and long history. As Rocklin (1996) observed,

> I imagine that people have been presenting others' work as their own at least since—well, at least since there have been people. Because students are people, I don't suppose any of us is surprised that some students sometimes present other people's work as their own. And, since we live in a market economy, I don't suppose any of us is surprised that some people have found ways to make money off the phenomenon.... People have been selling term papers at least since I started college almost 25 years ago. The nature of the market has evolved as technologies

have come along to facilitate it. When I was a student, most papers were locally produced and sold. Shortly after I graduated from college and started graduate school, posters started appearing on bulletin boards advertising catalogs of term papers. The advent of 800-number marketing techniques and the widespread use of credit cards... allowed for national markets in term papers. (p. 1)

It is not simply the persistence of this issue that should rally us to action; it is the recognition that there is a profound and critical relationship between integrity and our cultural values as institutions of higher education (see, e.g., Aaron, 1992; Burnett, Rudolph, & Clifford, 1998; Dalton, 1998; Drinan, 1999; Kibler, 1998; Peterson, 1988). Citing Peterson (1988), Aaron confirmed that cheating "conflicts with the core purposes of higher education: the search for knowledge and truth and the creation and communication of ideas" (1992, p. 107). And although we may disagree on things like contracts and curriculum, we higher education colleagues recognize that if we fail to identify, confront, and eliminate academic dishonesty from our midst, we risk our integrity. Without integrity, our constituencies have no reason to believe we are capable of fulfilling our mission:

The effects of failing to address academic dishonesty contribute to a broader problem: the public's growing lack of confidence in the academy as illustrated by such professor-bashing books as Anderson's (1992) *Imposters in the Temple*, Cahn's (1994) *Saints and Scamps: Ethics in Academia*, and Sykes's (1998) *ProfScam: Professors and the Demise of Higher Education*. Students who cheat, those who see others successfully cheat, those who hear others brag about how they cheated their way through college, and employers who find themselves with incompetent and dishonest employees cannot help but lose faith in academia. Such loss of faith can easily lead to loss of support for higher education. (Whitley & Keith-Spiegel, 2002)

Several researchers have noted the unusual silence with which the existence of academic dishonesty has been met, not only within community colleges, specifically, but also in 4-year colleges and universities. Alschuler and

Blimling (1995) observed, "The mystery is not why cheating is wrong or why students cheat, but why there is so little passion about this massive assault on the highest values of the academy. Why no high profile investigations, and emergency programs to restore academic integrity?" (p. 124). Others, however, have noted the scarcity of response to cheating. Aaron (1992), for example, noted, "The relatively low percentages of institutions with faculty and/or student development programs that specifically address the issue, and even smaller percentages that have conducted some form of internal study in regard to it, raise questions about the commitment to academic integrity" (p. 113).

Aaron, whose research encompassed both 2-year and 4-year institutions, also noted that

> Four-year collegiate institutions are significantly more likely to respond to the problem than community colleges. They are also more likely to possess specific adjudication procedures for acts of misconduct, more likely to use assessment and development programming to address the problem, and more likely to use campus media to enhance the issue's visibility on campus. (2002, p. 113)

The unique community college mission is the cornerstone of our institutions. It could be argued that it is precisely because of our mission that we are better poised to respond to the threat of academic dishonesty than those within traditional 4-year institutions. Consider, for example, the following:

- Community colleges are inextricably and purposefully grounded on an ethical and moral base of egalitarianism, equity, and integrity of purpose.
- Community colleges are equal partners in the higher education family, offering a variety of learning opportunities. As such, it is in our individual and collective best interests to ensure the integrity of our courses, certificates, and degrees.
- Community colleges place more emphasis on teaching and learning. They typically have smaller classes and provide more interaction between instructors and students, which puts them in an ideal situation to address occurrences of academic dishonesty.
- Community colleges have a well-earned reputation as being flexible and adaptable and, thus, poised to address new challenges.

- Unlike other institutions of higher education, community colleges are closely tied to the communities they reside in and serve. Maintaining the public confidence of our communities' demands that we seize the opportunity to offer value-added experiences to the learning process by addressing the character development of students and ensuring the integrity of teaching methods.

In *Dilemmas of Leadership: Decision Making in the Community College*, Vaughan (1992) confirmed the role that community colleges play in the intellectual and ethical development of their students, adding that "the mission of the community college is to be committed to actualizing people to their fullest as human beings. Colleges truly are about the business of helping people become the kind of people we would like to have in our own neighborhood" (p. 193).

But are we? We enroll millions of students, teach tens, if not hundreds, of millions of classes, and award grades that we trust reflect the extent to which our expected outcomes have been met. We engage, counsel, advise, encourage, and direct students. And they, in turn, we hope, accomplish their academic goals, gain employment, graduate, or transfer. We may even be improving our ability to demonstrate all that we do and embrace the twin concepts of institutional effectiveness and accountability. But, within the context of this issue, can we say that we have done all that is possible to safeguard our colleges (and the honest students within them) from the threat of academic dishonesty? Can we say that we know our students to be more (or less) honest than their 4-year counterparts? Have we done all we can to make ourselves familiar with the issue? Researched and implemented appropriate policies? Praised integrity? Sanctioned dishonesty? Can we say that grades we have given are untainted by false effort? Can we say that we have done all we possibly could to engage our learners where it is most important—in the classroom—and with conversation more engaging than a statement on a syllabus or a first-day handout? Have we raised with them the deeply held convictions of the culture of higher education? Have we designed learning experiences that reflect a synthesis of our most cherished beliefs such as authenticity of purpose, the inherent value of learning, and the honor of achievement, or have we silently observed the commoditization of higher education? And if we have, do we plan to continue? For how long?

As we have had so many times in our history as community colleges, we have a choice. We can garner our collective talent, will, and considerable intellectual heft and address these issues, or we can sit silently aside and watch the very institutions we dedicate our life's work to be tarnished by deceit. No doubt about it, there is nothing easy or simple about finding answers to these questions, but that is, at least in part, the purpose of this book. In the forthcoming chapters, I will familiarize readers with the issue of academic dishonesty; examine data that provide a benchmark for understanding students' attitudes, beliefs, and behaviors as they pertain to cheating; and highlight some leaders who have already begun their journey toward the resolution of this epidemic.

CHAPTER TWO

Defining Academic Dishonesty and Assessing Its Prevalence

Definition and Characteristics of Academic Dishonesty

In chapter 1, I noted that the lack of a commonly agreed-upon definition of academic dishonesty has contributed to the difficulty of measuring and assessing it. A number of researchers have addressed this lack in their work (e.g., Barnett & Dalton, 1981; Bricault, 1998; Dalton, 1998; Fass, 1986; Hollinger & Lanza-Kaduce, 1996; Kaplin & Lee, 1995; Kibler, 1998; Nuss, 1984; Pavela, 1978; Rafetto, 1985; Singhal & Johnson, 1983; Stern & Havlicek, 1986; Whitley & Keith-Spiegel, 2002).

Fass (1986), for example, noted the difficulty involved in formulating policy in the absence of a working definition of academic dishonesty:

> Most colleges and universities have very little written in their handbooks or catalogs about the kinds of behavior that constitute cheating. The blatant forms of cheating, such as copying another student's answers on a test, using crib sheets or other aids that have been explicitly prohibited, or submitting a paper that is copied in its entirety from a published work do not require description or elaboration. Beyond such obvious examples, however, statements about academic ethics are difficult to formulate; the process of doing so requires a painstaking discussing and analysis of an institution's traditions and values.... Attempts to define academic dishonesty are often couched in terms such as "taking unfair advantage of other students" or "representing the words or ideas of theirs as one's own." Common understandings of these concepts do not exist on many campuses, however, and institutions should try to provide clearer definitions for the guidance of students and faculty. (p. 33)

Fass provided examples of specific issues that clearer definitions are needed for, such as using other students' work as resources or incorporating the guidance obtained from a tutor (see Fass, 1986, pp. 33–34).

More recently, Kibler (1998) stated that "one of the most significant problems associated with a literature review of academic dishonesty is the absence of a generally accepted definition of the subject" (p. 24). Offering a historical review of what others have suggested as working definitions, Kibler noted that "academic dishonesty usually refers to forms of cheating and plagiarism that result in students giving or receiving unauthorized assistance in an academic exercise or receiving credit for work that is not their own" (p. 24), but he added that other unethical practices included obtaining copies of tests, using unauthorized notes, working together with other students without authorization, using crib sheets and stolen exams, changing grades and answers, and using an instructor's manual.

Bricault (1998) stated that "there is not universal agreement over what constitutes academic dishonesty: what some call cheating, others call collaboration" (p. 2). He added,

> Trying to provide a succinct definition of academic dishonesty is a challenge, given its many facets. Some educators rely on legal or dictionary definitions; others fall back on metaphors and analogies. I would like to examine the various forms of misconduct, which will lead to a composite definition of academic dishonesty. When dishonesty in the classroom is discussed, most teachers and students think first of cheating, "a fraud committed by deception; a trick, imposition, or imposture" (*The New Webster*, 971, p. 140). Cheating has been aptly termed "the academic equivalent of urban crime" (Alschuler & Blimling, 1995) and encompasses a laundry list of unacceptable behavior, such as 'copying or attempting to copy from another student's work [or] using or attempting to use unauthorized information, notes [and] study aids (Oakton Community College, 1977). (Bricault, 1998, p. 2)

Before turning to a review of the research on the prevalence of academic dishonesty, I offer a working definition—based on the work of Pavela (1978) and Whitley and Keith-Spiegel (2002)—and a list of behaviors and activities typically exhibited by students engaged in academic dishonesty (derived from Maramark & Maline, 1993, based on questionnaires and surveys used in studies of academic dishonesty).

A Working Definition of Academic Dishonesty

1. *Cheating.* Intentionally using unauthorized materials, information, or study aids in any work submitted for credit (e.g., using crib notes, copying another's work during tests, or collaborating with others on out-of-class assignments without permission).
2. *Fabrication.* Intentionally falsifying or misrepresenting information derived from another source in an assignment (e.g., making up sources for the bibliography of a paper or faking the results of a laboratory assignment).
3. *Plagiarism.* Deliberately adopting or reproducing ideas, words, or statements of another person as one's own with acknowledgment (e.g., turning in a paper written by another student, buying a paper from a commercial source, failing to properly attribute quotations within a paper, or submitting the same paper for credit in more than one course without the instructor's permission [self-plagiarism]).
4. *Facilitating academic dishonesty.* Intentionally helping another engage in academic dishonesty.
5. *Misrepresentation.* Providing false information to an instructor concerning an academic exercise (e.g., giving a false excuse for missing a test or deadline or falsely claiming to have submitted a paper).
6. *Failure to contribute.* Taking credit for participation in a collaborative project while failing to do one's fair share.
7. *Sabotage.* Preventing others from completing their work (e.g., disturbing someone's lab experiment or removing materials from a reserved reading file so that others cannot use them).

Behaviors and Activities Associated With Academic Dishonesty

- Copying from another student's exam.
- Taking an exam from someone else.
- Purchasing term papers and turning them in as original work.
- Copying materials without citing the original source.
- Padding entries on a bibliography.
- Feigning illness to avoid a test.
- Submitting the same term paper to another class without permission.

- Studying a copy of an exam before taking a makeup exam.
- Giving another student answers during an exam.
- Reviewing previous copies of an instructor's test.
- Using notes or books during an exam when prohibited.
- Reviewing stolen copies of an exam.
- Turning in a lab report without doing the experiment.
- Sabotaging someone else's work (on a disk, in a lab, etc.).
- Failing to report grading errors.
- Collaborating on homework or take-home exams when instructions called for independent work.
- Giving test questions to students in another class.
- Sharing answers during an exam by using signals.
- Developing a relationship with an instructor to get test information.
- Plagiarizing.
- Studying tests or used term papers from fraternity or sorority files.
- Engaging in bribery or blackmail.
- Attempting to bias an instructor's grading after an exam.
- Writing papers for another student.
- Hiring a ghostwriter.
- Altering or forging an official university document.

The Prevalence of Academic Dishonesty

For the past four decades, especially since the 1980s, researchers have studied academic dishonesty from several different perspectives. Many have obtained baseline rates of cheating from students' self-reports. Others have sought to identify the traits and characteristics of students who are most likely to be engaged in cheating. Some have compared instructors' and students' perceptions of cheating, and some have examined the issue from a broader perspective so that they can investigate whether organizational factors may deter academic dishonesty or promote integrity. Finally, some researchers have been focusing on the effect of new technologies on the occurrence or prevalence of cheating.

There is evidence to suggest that academic dishonesty predates the research of the past four decades. Maramark and Maline found evidence dating to the 1930s. In 1993, they stated, "For more than 50 years, we have been warned of a problem that threatens the foundation of higher education: students' lack of appreciation for integrity in the quest of truth and knowledge" (p. 3). Perhaps because the designs and populations of extant studies on academic dishonesty have differed substantially, they have yielded prevalence rates spanning a wide range. Maramark and Maline reported that "cheating among college students range(s) anywhere from 9% to 95%" (1993, p. 3) and cited sampling techniques and sample sizes, design strategies, types of cheating and cheating measures, and types of institutions as possible reasons for the variation.

The wide range of variation is also illustrated in a survey of prevalence rates conducted by Davis, Grover, Becker, and McGregor (1992). According to one early study (Drake, 1941), the rate of cheating was once thought to be no more than 23%. In 1960, Goldsen, Rosenberg, William, and Suchman reported rates of 38% and 49% for 1952 and 1960, respectively. Subsequently, other researchers reported rates of cheating between 64% and 76% (Baird, 1980; Bowers, 1964; Hetherington & Feldman, 1964). In 1989, Jendrek placed the rate between 40% and 60%; within the same decade, rates as high as 82% (Stern & Havlicek, 1986) and 88% (Sierles, Hendricks, & Circle, 1980) were cited. Davis (1993) observed not only that academic dishonesty has been a perennial problem but also that efforts to address it in the research have lagged behind perception of the problem:

> Despite the fact that reports of academically dishonest practices have appeared for over 60 years, concerted research efforts appear to have been mounted only during the past two decades. This recent surge of interest may be attributed to the fact that some educators, such as Singhal (1982), feel that "cheating has become one of the major problems in education today." (p. 2)

In the past two decades that Davis alluded to—the 1980s and 1990s—researchers have reported high prevalence rates. The following findings emerged from one survey of the literature:

- 87% of students had cheated at least once (Scheers & Dayton, 1987).
- 23% to 88% of students had cheated (Davis et al., 1992).
- More than 80% of students had cheated (Generoux & McLeod, 1995).
- Cheating increased from 54.1% in 1984 to 61.2% in 1994 (Diekhoff et al., 1996). (Roberts, Anderson, & Yanish, 1997).

The Relation Between Academic Dishonesty and Ethics

Around 1990, Donald L. McCabe, a professor of management at Rutgers University and founder of the Center for Academic Integrity began to explore academic dishonesty from a new perspective. As faculty members and student affairs administrators, McCabe and his colleagues (including Kenneth Butterfield, Sally Cole, Linda Klebe Treviño, and Gary Pavela) were interested in the ethical orientations of those who would someday inherit positions of leadership within business and industry. McCabe, Klebe Treviño, and Butterfield (2001) wrote,

> We have expended considerable time trying to understand the ethical inclinations of tomorrow's business leaders—students majoring in business and those majoring in other subjects who intend to pursue a career in business. To understand how the ethics and ethical development of these future businesspeople are similar to, or differ from, those pursuing other career choices, we have also studied the ethical inclinations of college students in general. (p. 220)

McCabe and his colleagues surveyed research findings brought to light in the early 1990s and, recognizing the lack of large-scale, multi-campus, multi-variable studies, initiated their own research agenda:

> The ... result [of previous research] has been a series of studies that have advanced our understanding of why college students cheat, provided administrators and faculty with a broader set of tools that can be used to curb cheating on college campuses, and helped foster academic integrity in American colleges and universities (McCabe, 1992, 1993; McCabe and Klebe Treviño, 1993, 1997; McCabe et. al., 1996, 1999). Not least among the outcomes of this work was the formation of the Center for Academic Integrity in 1992, a consortium of more than 200 colleges and universities united in a common effort to initiate and maintain a dialogue among students, faculty, and administrators on the issue of academic integrity. (McCabe et al., 2001, pp. 221–222)

The research agenda that McCabe and his colleagues adopted yielded the following:

- Students who engage in acts of academic dishonesty "neutralize" their behavior by denying culpability or wrong-doing or diminishing the effect of their behavior on others (McCabe, 1992).
- A relationship exists between cheating and peer behavior (McCabe, 1993).
- Many faculty members do not respond to student academic dishonesty with the level of severity that students may have anticipated (McCabe, 1993).
- Students with a tendency to commit acts of academic dishonesty tend to migrate toward lenient teachers and away from those who pursue prevention and punishment (McCabe, 1993).
- Less cheating occurs in colleges that have honor codes (McCabe, 1993).
- To be effective, honor codes must be authentic in words as well as deeds; in other words, simply implementing an honor code is not enough to cause the kind of cultural change that will truly diminish dishonest academic behaviors (McCabe, 1993).
- Honor codes can have an effect on behavior that exceeds students' traditional education and that extends into their professional careers (McCabe, Klebe Treviño, & Butterfield, 1996).
- Cheating tends to be more prevalent on larger campuses (McCabe & Klebe Treviño, 1997, p. 223).
- Men report higher amounts of academic dishonesty than do women, but women in nontraditional majors tend to reveal greater levels of dishonesty than do women in general (McCabe & Klebe Treviño, 1997).
- Students with productive grade point averages (GPAs) report less cheating than students with nonproductive GPAs (McCabe & Klebe Treviño, 1997).
- Students and researchers agree on many of the behaviors necessary to diminish cheating (McCabe & Pavela, 1997; McCabe, Klebe Treviño, & Butterfield, 1999).
- Students in colleges that have honor codes internalize academic integrity differently than do other students and have less difficulty avoiding cheating (McCabe et al., 1999).
- An analysis of context factors (i.e., peer cheating behavior, peer disapproval of cheating behavior, and perceived severity of penalties for cheating) versus individual factors (i.e., age, gender, GPA, and

participation in extracurricular activities) and their influence on cheating behaviors "pointed to the primacy of the institutional context in influencing cheating behavior" (McCabe et al., 2001, p. 222; see also McCabe & Klebe Treviño, 1997).

Founded by Donald McCabe, the Center for Academic Integrity (CAI; see www.academicintegrity.org) has conducted several large-scale research studies focusing on the prevalence of academic dishonesty, but it has also pursued other research paths, including analysis of faculty's and students' perceptions and of the effect of honor codes on diminishing cheating behavior. Additionally, CAI offers individual and organizational memberships, hosts annual conferences, acknowledges best practices, recognizes "integrity champions," and offers research fellowships. Through "integrity audits," CAI offers member colleges and universities a means of objectively measuring and reporting specific behaviors and perceptions of students and faculty so that CAI can determine the extent to which they reflect a culture of integrity. It should be noted, however, that the majority of members are 4-year institutions.

By 2005, academic dishonesty was described as an epidemic that permeated the education system, an epidemic fueled by factors such as a general sense of ethical decline, easy access to technology, an increasingly competitive economic environment, and the pervasive belief that we are all entitled to "the good life." Those factors have their parallel in cheating beyond academe. For example, researchers examining corporate scandals in which numerous acts of deceit have occurred commonly refer to a phenomenon known as the "fraud triangle"—a rubric applied by business and industry to better understand the circumstances under which an otherwise moral person gives in to the temptation to commit acts of outright dishonesty. Described by Wolfe and Hermanson (2005) as the presence of an incentive or pressure, the opportunity to effect the act, and the ability to rationalize the transgression, the fraud triangle can also be applied to understanding dishonesty in an academic context.

About 30 years ago, Houston (1976) noted the apparent ethical "slide" occurring among students, which was typified by the belief that "everyone cheats" (p. 301). Similarly, Baird (1980) noted that students perceived cheating to be a normal occurrence. Later, Aaron and Georgia (1994) identified this moral malaise as an "an ethical deterioration" (p. 84) and, to support their thesis, cited both the Carnegie Council on Policy Studies in Higher Education (1979) and the Carnegie Foundation for the Advancement of Teaching (1990) which "...

contended that student academic integrity had continued to erode on today's 'anything goes' campus ..." (Aaron & Georgia, 1994, p. 83). This sentiment was echoed by Dalton (1998), who pointed to "the utilitarian and materialistic values of contemporary college students" (p. 2) and noted,

> The longitudinal data on first time in college students ... indicates a long trend line of increasing concern about money and status among college students and declining interest in education for its own intrinsic personal worth. Although the materialistic interests of college students have begun to level off in recent years (Astin, 1994), it is clear that the overriding priorities of today's college students are to regard higher education as a gateway to future financial and status rewards. Moreover, economic downsizing and increasing competition for jobs and access to graduate and professional schools have fueled the pressure for good grades and academic success among today's college students. (p. 2)

Increasing numbers of students demonstrate the ability to commit a variety of dishonest acts while continuing to characterize themselves as moral people. For example, a study conducted by the Josephson Institute of Ethics (2004) showed that nearly two thirds of the nation's high school students surveyed had cheated on exams (62%), more than one in four (27%) had stolen from a store within the past 12 months, and 40% admitted that they "sometimes lie to save money" (p. 1). At the same time, "the majority of the students reported high self-appraisals of their character (74% rated their own ethic higher than those of their peers)" and that they "stated their convictions that honesty, ethics, and good character are very important (almost all, 98%, said it is important for them to be a person of good character)" (p. 1). The report continued,

> What's more, most have unrealistically high self-images when it comes to ethics. Asked "if people you know were asked to list the most ethical people they know, how many would put you on their lists?" 83% said at least half the people they know would list them. Additionally, 92% said they were satisfied with their ethics and character.... The inconsistency seems to be explained by high levels of cynicism about the ethics of successful people

and the prevalence of cheating in the "real world" creating a justification for dishonest conduct. Cynicism is especially strong in young males. Two-thirds indicated a belief that "in the real world, successful people do what they have to do to win, even if others consider it cheating"—and more than half (52%) of the females agreed with this cynical assessment. In addition, half (51%) of the males agreed with: "A person has to lie or cheat sometimes in order to succeed." About one-third of the female students expressed a similar view. (Josephson Institute, 2004, p. 1)

According to Michael Josephson, president of the Josephson Institute of Ethics, the news, despite the findings of the study, is not all bad. He added his analysis of the study's findings, part promising and part perturbing:

Though the Report Card on the Integrity of American Youth continues to contain failing grades, there is reason for hope. For the first time in 12 years, the cheating and theft rates have actually dipped downward, and the stated devotion to ethics is the strongest we've seen. While this results in a troubling inconsistency between words and actions, character education efforts should be able to build on the fundamental appreciation of ethics, character, and trust to achieve continuing improvements in conduct. Still, it can't be comforting to know that the majority of the next generation of police officers, politicians, accountants, lawyers, doctors, nuclear inspectors, and journalists are entering the workforce as unrepentant cheaters. (cited in Josephson Institute, 2004, pp. 1–2)

Research Focusing on Community Colleges

It took almost three decades for researchers to address the prevalence of academic dishonesty specifically in the community college context. Part of the reason for this delay is obvious: In 1964, when Bowers published the results of his seminal work, the nation's community colleges were just being born. Nonetheless, among the hundreds of studies on academic dishonesty that now exist, relatively few encompass or focus specifically on community colleges (e.g., Aaron, 1992; Aaron & Georgia, 1994; Burke, 1997; Gerdeman, 2000; Lumsden & Arvidson, 2001; Moeck, 1999, 2002; Smyth & Davis, 2003). The findings of those researchers did little to paint a more optimistic picture.

Aaron (1992) sought to discover whether colleges were addressing academic dishonesty. For his study, he surveyed a random sample of 257 chief student affairs officers at 4-year public and 4-year private colleges and universities and at community colleges nationwide. In comparing percentages for the three types of institutions combined with those for three types of institutions individually, he identified a number of potentially troubling issues specific to 2-year colleges:

- Four-year public (70%) and private (72.4%) colleges were significantly more likely than were community colleges (20.9%) to have guidelines specifically for adjudicating academic dishonesty; they were also much more likely than community colleges to disseminate information on academic integrity in a brochure.

- Across all college types, less than 8% reported that their faculty members address academic dishonesty through classroom discussion or syllabi. The rate was highest for public 4-year colleges (10.9%) and lowest for community colleges (2.3%).

- More than 21% used no specific method for disseminating information about academic dishonesty to faculty members; 25% of community colleges lacked a specific method.

- At 35.7% of all institutions, chief student affairs officers were responsible for adjudication procedures, compared to 76.2% at community colleges and 20.5% at private 4-year colleges.

- Academic affairs officers were more likely to have adjudication authority at 4-year public and private colleges (48.2% and 42.5%, respectively) than at community colleges (11.9%).

- Only 16% of all institutions offered student development programs focusing on academic dishonesty. The percentage was highest for private 4-year colleges (24.6%) and lowest for community colleges (4.7%).

- Only 15.2% of all institutions had made an effort to assess the extent of academic dishonesty on their campuses through an internal survey or study of faculty or students. Whereas the percentage of 4-year public and private universities making an effort ranged from 18% to 19%, respectively, only 4.7% of the community colleges had tackled this issue. (Aaron, 1992, pp. 108–113)

In summary, 4-year institutions are significantly more likely than community colleges to respond to academic dishonesty, to have adjudication procedures, to use assessment and development programming to address the problem, and to use campus media to enhance the issue's visibility.

Using a similar design (i.e., comparing and contrasting 4-year public and private colleges and universities with community colleges), Aaron and Georgia (1994) analyzed the perceptions of college administrators. As in Aaron's 1992 study, they sampled 257 chief student affairs officers (including chief academic officers) across the country and measured the responses to 10 questions divided into three categories: faculty behavior, institutional response, and student behavior and classroom environment. Their findings indicate a combination of good news and bad news for community colleges:

- More than 60% stated that faculty members are most likely to handle incidents in their own way and not as suggested by institutional guidelines.
- More than 40% thought that most faculty members were unaware of guidelines for handling academic dishonesty (from a high of 54.3% at 4-year public institutions to a low of 27.9% at community colleges).
- Most respondents (62.1%) indicated that most faculty members define plagiarism and cheating to students during the first class and explained how violations would be treated. A significant difference was found between the three institutional types, however, ranging from almost 75% of respondents at community colleges to a low of 49.3% at 4-year public institutions.
- Slightly more than half agreed that their institutions had made "an extensive commitment to addressing student academic dishonesty on campus." Responses ranged from a high of 66.7% at private institutions to a low of 39.5% at community colleges.
- Less than 37% supported the idea of designating an official grade to denote failure in a course as a result of academic dishonesty. Support was highest at 4-year private institutions (46.3%) and lowest at community colleges (25.6%).
- Two thirds of the respondents agreed that "cheating increases when students perceive tests or grading practices to be unfair." Responses ranged from a high of 76.4% at 4-year private institutions to a low of 53.5% at community colleges.

- Close to two thirds also agreed that "the likelihood that any given students will be dishonest increases to the extent that fellow classmates cheat." A statistically significant difference was found between institutional types, ranging from a high of 82.1% at private institutions to a low of 41.8% at community colleges.
- The consensus (72.8%) was that "students look the other way when they see someone cheat," slightly higher at 4-year institutions (79.7%) and lower at community colleges (61.3%).
- When asked if plagiarism might be the result of lack of understanding, 52.9% at 4-year public institutions and 38.6% at private institutions agreed, compared to 52.3% at community colleges.
- Only slightly more than one third of all respondents indicated an association between poor teaching and student cheating: 46.3% at private 4-year institutions, 27.5% at 4-year public institutions, and 31% at community colleges. (Aaron & Georgia, 1994, pp. 85–87)

Several conclusions were drawn from the findings of this study, not the least of which was the confirmation that "there is a general consensus that student academic dishonesty is a large and pervasive problem and that colleges… have not yet addressed it adequately" (Aaron & Georgia, 1994, p. 90). Additionally, Aaron and Georgia pointed out that administrators tended to agree more than disagree about the nature and extent of the problem, and that each institution must approach the problem in its own way, depending on how the problem presents itself on campus and on the resources available for dealing with it.

Focusing on Faculty's Perceptions and Attitudes

Burke (1997) framed his inquiry from within a multi-campus community college, examining five variables: faculty perceptions of the extent of academic honesty; perceptions of, and attitudes toward, academic dishonesty, policy, and policy implementation; responses to academic dishonesty; attitudes concerning values education; and attitudes about responsibility for reducing academic dishonesty. The majority of the faculty members (53% of all faculty within the college) responding to his survey were part-time instructors (56%) teaching during the day (63%); 40% of them had been at the college 5–11 years.

Burke's study yielded the surprising finding that "academic dishonesty appears to occur infrequently and not to be a pressing concern" (1997, p. 60). However, further analysis of the statistical data revealed a variance based on faculty type: "full-time faculty perceive the problem to be more serious than do their part-time colleagues" (p. 62). Additionally, Burke's research suggested that faculty members with more experience (5–11 years) perceived academic dishonesty to be more problematic than did new members of the faculty. Similarly, he noted that perceptions differed between campuses within the same district and from one discipline to another. For example, humanities, math, and science faculty members reported greater concern about the academic dishonesty problem than did social science and developmental studies faculty members.

Faculty members indicated that they believe they were familiar with their college's policy on academic dishonesty and did not perceive policy implementation as being time-consuming or adversarial or penalties as being inappropriate, agreeing only slightly that academic freedom, personal liability, and teaching reputation were concerns. The majority agreed that a primary role of the college faculty is to teach values and that the faculty should teach the importance of academic integrity. When asked about instances of academic dishonesty in their classrooms, 20% said they had not suspected instances, 35% had not encountered actual instances, and only small percentages had ignored academic dishonesty—7% in suspected cases and 2% in actual cases (Burke, 1997, p. 74). Looked at another way, the data show that 80% of faculty members had suspected academic dishonesty in their classes and that 65% had been certain of it. It is within this context that their original perception—that academic dishonesty is not a serious problem—is somewhat startling.

It is also significant to note that the faculty revealed a relatively generous level of professional discretion in confronting academic dishonesty. Burke observed,

> The most common response among faculty participants is to handle the incident with the student one-to-one (suspected, 48%; certain, 37%). Suspected academic dishonesty led to 31 percent of faculty giving the student a warning and 14 percent lowering the grade on the item in question. When faculty are certain of the occurrence of academic dishonesty, fewer choose a warning to the student (17%) and more choose to lower the item grade (25%). An "F" was assigned for the course by 2% of faculty who suspected academic dishonesty while 8% choose this response when certain. It appears that when faculty suspect that cheating or plagiarism has occurred, they are more likely to

take informal, non-punitive measures such as confronting the student or giving a warning. When suspicion becomes certainty, however, faculty become more willing to lower the grade. (1997, p. 76)

Burke's findings also seem to confirm the findings of other researchers (e.g., McCabe, 1993; Nuss, 1984; Singhal, 1982) who have observed that many faculty members often overlook cheating altogether to avoid involvement or do not report cheating to administrators:

Reporting incidents of academic dishonesty does not often occur among faculty participants. Ten percent report suspected academic dishonesty to the department chair while 16% report to the department chair when confronted with certain cheating or plagiarism. Even less likely is the chance that faculty report academic dishonesty to the dean of students (2%, suspected, 7% certain). Though the college policy indicates this response as a procedural matter, it is not common among the faculty respondents. (Burke, 1997, pp. 76–77)

Although there may be many valid reasons for the faculty not getting involved, one of the most unfortunate may be the apparent lack of trust that often exists between instructional and student services administration—a situation that is often exacerbated when the two functions are organizationally divided between separate administrators. Trust and support are also relevant in that, without them, the faculty may be deterred from seeking assistance with handling incidents of academic dishonesty. Perhaps instructors fear that reporting an act of cheating is an automatic indictment of their teaching skills. Perhaps they assume that the student cheating is hurting only himself or herself or that the distraction of being involved in the disciplinary process is not worth the required time and effort.

It should be noted that in those instances when a college has an academic integrity policy in place, faculty members who take it upon themselves to act outside the prescribed processes may well expose both the institution and themselves to allegations of violation of due process. This action is particularly dangerous. According to Gehring and Pavela (1994), those who fail to follow the processes outlined in an existing policy may be interpreted as acting outside the scope of their position and may jeopardize their expectation of legal counsel if the situation were to deteriorate into litigation.

Like other researchers, Gerdeman (2000) acknowledged the lack of research specific to community colleges but suggested that findings from studies of 4-year colleges and universities were relevant for community colleges. He reviewed research on topics such as frequency of behavior, factors associated with dishonesty, and responses of the faculty. Basing his recommendations on the conclusions drawn by Aaron (1992), he encouraged college leaders to "establish an environment where dishonesty is viewed as unacceptable and where any possible benefits are outweighed by risks of being caught and peer disapproval" (p. 4). Drawing upon prior research (e.g., Burke, 1997; Kerkvliet & Sigmund, 1999; McCabe & Klebe Treviño, 1996; Whitley, 1998), he suggested that community colleges take the following five steps:

1. Communicate policies on academic misconduct to students and faculty. Regular communication through a variety of media (e.g., handbooks, orientations, programs, and course materials) conveys the message that academic integrity is an important institutional priority.
2. Encourage the faculty to discuss dishonesty with students. Faculty comments reinforce and remind students of unacceptable behavior.
3. Establish nonpermissive examination environments. Watchful instructors, spaced seating, and varied exam formats are effective deterrents.
4. Apply consequences in a consistent, fair, and timely manner. Inconsistent and unpredictable responses to dishonesty erode student support for existing policies.
5. Maintain an environment of trust and honor. An emphasis on mature behavior, individual responsibility, and proper conduct enhances academic integrity. (Gerdeman, 2000, p. 4)

Others have stepped forward to address academic dishonesty in the community college, thus providing a snapshot of the status quo as well as advice for the future. Moeck (2002) suggested that "as members of the community college family, students, faculty members, and administrative staff assume a number of solemn responsibilities" (p. 488). Within the contextual framework of the roles and responsibilities of those constituents, Moeck added that "the institution is obligated to make certain that students have been informed about the negative aspects of cheating such as definitions, methods, concepts, and sanctions concerning academic dishonesty" (p. 489). More specifically, he pointed out that community college faculty and administrative staff "have a duty to communicate a personal philosophy on cheating, serve as role models of integrity, and directly confront students suspected of plagiarism or any form of cheating" (p. 489). But his passionate conclusions also extend to the students we serve:

> Students in community colleges assume the responsibility to keep current with course readings and assignments, to respect other's opinions, to show courtesy to other students as well as the instructor, and to provide open communication regarding attendance and promptness. Above all, students have an obligation to do their own work. They should know that any form of academic dishonesty will be acknowledged [and] documented, and that students will be held accountable for their actions and disciplined according to institutional policy. Sanctions can include "prosecution, dismissal, and/or a performance grade of 'F' for an examination, the particular assignment, or the entire course." (Moeck, 1999, p. 19)

> Community college students deserve forthright instructions concerning academic standards, student conduct, and ethical expectations. They should be discouraged from perpetrating academic dishonesty. Academic dishonesty hurts everyone. Simply, cheating is theft; plagiarism is forgery; collusion and complicity are conspiracy. These acts are all crimes. The consequences of committing a crime is punishment. (Moeck, 2002, p. 489)

Focusing on Students' Attitudes and Behaviors

Whitley and Keith-Spiegel (2002) examined characteristics of students who admitted to engaging in academic dishonesty and sought correlations in five categories: demographic factors, academic characteristics, beliefs and perceptions, personality, and behavior. For the 40 characteristics they studied across those categories, they found strong correlations between academic dishonesty and the following six beliefs, perceptions, and behaviors:

- Have moderate expectations for success.
- Have favorable attitudes toward academic dishonesty.

- Perceive that social norms allow dishonesty.
- Anticipate high reward for success.
- Have cheated in the past.
- Party more frequently. (p. 31)

They also found moderate correlations for 10 characteristics, 6 of which were classified as academic characteristics or beliefs and perceptions:

- Are younger.
- Are unmarried.
- Perform less well in the course.
- Report having high academic workloads.
- Are faced with important outcomes.
- Report feeling pressure to get high grades.
- Feel little moral obligation not to cheat.
- Perceive greater competition for grades.
- Perceive a high benefit-to-risk ratio for dishonest behavior.
- Show a general pattern of mildly deviant behavior. (p. 31)

Other researchers have turned their attention to analyzing variables that might explain the individual, social, and organizational factors that contribute to academic dishonesty. Gerdeman (2000), for example, divided the factors associated with academic dishonesty into four categories: (a) individual characteristics, (b) peer group influences, (c) instructor influences, and (d) institutional policies. His observations provide a reasonably comprehensive review of the studies that have focused their efforts in this direction. It is significant to note that Gerdeman's review includes the results of one study specific to community college students (Antion & Michael, 1983)—a rarity that Lumsden and Arvidson (2001) pointed out:

> The wealth of information regarding academic integrity, honesty, and dishonesty at the four-year level, for both private and public institutions, is extraordinary. However, significantly more study is required at community colleges, as the composition of the student population has typically included more diversity. A search of the ERIC database from 1970 to 2001 and the PsychLIT database from 1985 to 2001 yielded just one study

specific to community college students' cheating behaviors (i.e., Antion and Michael, 1983) as well as another study whose student sample was 30% community college students (Graham, Monday, O'Brien, and Steffen, 1994). (p. 1)

Lumsden and Arvidson summarized the results of exploratory research conducted within a large, multicampus community college district in a metropolitan area with 89 students responding to an adapted version of the survey provided by the Center for Academic Integrity. Although Lumsden and Arvidson acknowledged that the size of the sample and the lack of a randomized process provide an insufficient basis to draw generalizable conclusions, their findings provide a significant, if not reliable, benchmark. Most of the responses seem to reveal extremely virtuous community college students. According to their answers,

- 68% never copied from other students during a test without their knowledge, and 74% never copied from other students during a test without their permission.
- 84% never used prohibited crib notes during a test; 60% never obtained questions or answers from someone who had already taken a test.
- 67% never helped someone else cheat on a test; 81% never cheated on a test in any way.
- 81% never turned in work done by someone else; 83% never wrote or provided a paper for another student.
- 82% never fabricated or falsified a bibliography; 60% had copied a few sentences of material without footnoting them.
- 71% never received substantial, forbidden help on their assignments; 53% never worked on an assignment with others when the instructor had asked for individual work.
- 85% never turned in a paper based on information obtained from a term paper mill or Web site; 78% never plagiarized a paper in any way using the Internet as a source.
- 85% never copied another student's program in a course requiring computer work.
- 88% never falsified laboratory or research data. (Lumsden & Arvidson, 2001, p. 3)

Similarly, when asked about the conditions most likely to influence their decision to commit acts of academic dishonesty, students cited the following:

- The likelihood of getting caught.
- The pressure to get good grades.
- The penalties for cheating.
- The pressure associated with getting behind in one's schoolwork; workload at school.
- The school's policy on academic integrity.
- Whether they think what they are contemplating is wrong.

The fact that others cheat in community college classes was not a deciding factor for most students (Lumsden & Arvidson, 2001, pp. 3-4).

Those who have confronted this particular form of mischief or who have familiarized themselves with the findings of national studies of 4-year college students may read with no small amount of incredulity the results outlined in this study. Further, they may brook considerable reservations regarding the "tentative conclusions" set forth by the researcher, which suggest that "the majority of community college students do not engage in academic dishonesty" and "the fear of being caught is the primary deterrent to academic misconduct among community college students" (Lumsden & Arvidson, 2001). However, it is significant to note that the researchers themselves caution against generalizing the results and emphasize the need for a broader sample with an emphasis on community college students. They wrote,

> The study we have reported here begs for replication. Our results diverge dramatically from the findings of Graham, et al. (1994), so further examination of cheating behaviors at the community college level is clearly indicated.... Ideally, the need is for a national study of a large, randomly selected sample of community college students. Our study was exploratory in nature; which means our findings are not necessarily generaliz-able, and our conclusions are tentative at best. (pp. 4–5)

In 2003, Smyth and Davis turned their attention to academic dishonesty in an article titled *An Examination of Student Cheating in the Two-Year College.* They reported the results of a survey conducted within a 2-year institution and with a sample size three times larger than that used in previous research, but using a survey design different from that used by Lumsden and Arvidson (2001). The results provide an additional, much-needed glimpse into the behaviors and perceptions of community college students. Specifically, they discovered the following:

- 61.4% of the respondents believed that less cheating occurred in college than in high school; the 38.6% who thought cheating levels were the same or higher in college represents a relatively high percentage given the youth of the students and the fact that they spent less time in community college than in high school.
- More than 82% of students reported seeing cheating occur, compared to 18% who had not; 43.2% never observed the detection of cheating in their classrooms.
- A little less than half (45.6%) reported that they had cheated in college at least once, comparable to the 49.77% found by Grimes (2002) in a study of undergraduates at a major state university.
- Almost 90% of the respondents feared punishment if caught (Smyth & Davis, 2003, pp. 7–8).

Exploring correlations between behaviors and demographics, Smyth and Davis found the following:

- Although 66% of the students reported having been asked by another student to cheat, only 24% admitted that they would assist other students in cheating.
- There is a statistically significant difference between the percentages of of full-time versus part-time students who have been asked to cheat, with full-time students reporting a higher incidence.
- Nearly all respondents believed that cheating is ethically wrong (92%), but 45% found cheating to be socially acceptable.
- Of students living off campus, 95% assessed cheating as unethical, compared to 85% of dormitory residents—a statistically significant difference. Similarly, off-campus students believed cheating to be less socially acceptable (41%) than did dormitory residents (55%).
- Differences for classes and genders were also statistically significant: 51% of sophomores found cheating to be socially acceptable compared to only 39% of freshmen, and 55% of male students versus 39% of female students believed that cheating is socially acceptable. (Smyth & Davis, 2003, pp. 9–10)

When Smyth and Davis compared the data for those who report having cheated and those who have not, the results yielded the following:

> In analyzing the students who have admitted to cheating, 96% of them report to having seen cheating, 63% report having seen cheating detected, 90% of them fear punishment if caught, 88% think it is ethically wrong, and 58% think it is socially acceptable.... Of the students who report having not cheated, only 70% report having observed cheating. It is also surprising that cheaters observe more classroom detection of cheating (63% vs. 51%), yet still they commit such acts. It is possible that those students who cheat are either more likely to look for similar, reinforcing behavior from their peers or are simply interested in the art of cheating and thus are on the lookout for new and innovative techniques. However, it is important to note that both groups fear punishment the same (90% vs. 89%), suggesting that the need to cheat overrides both the fear factor and the lessons to be learned from observing others being caught in the acts. (2003, p. 10)

Perhaps the most significant finding of this study was set forth in the summary. Here, the authors noted, "Almost 74% of the respondents observed collegiate cheating, 43% have witnessed the detection of cheating, and 45.6% have confessed to cheating at least once" (2003, p. 12). Furthermore, they identified a paradox common to the findings of others who have noted the apparent lack of cognitive dissonance among those who identify cheating as morally wrong, but socially acceptable. They wrote,

> Although a substantially high percentage of all respondents agree that cheating is ethically wrong, it is disappointing that nearly half of the respondents find cheating to be socially acceptable. The average of the male responses regarding the acceptability of cheating is significantly higher than is the female response average. Similarly, the proportion of sophomores [who] consider cheating to be socially acceptable is significantly larger than the proportion of freshmen who voice this opinion. (2003, p. 12)

What conclusions, if any, might be made based on those findings? More, perhaps, than might be imagined at first glance. Consider, for example, the finding that relatively high percentages of community college students—unlike their 4-year counterparts—fear being caught. This piece of information is helpful for faculty and administrators alike. For faculty, it indicates that efforts to communicate the value of integrity and the chances of being caught will not fall on deaf ears. For administrators, it affirms the need to punctuate the awareness with appropriate policies and processes to address those who are caught and protect those who are virtuous.

Next, consider the finding that 43% of community college students versus 90% of 4-year students have witnessed the detection of cheating. This result may suggest that community college faculty members are either more vigilant or more successful at catching cheaters or that they are perceived to be by students. However, the reported levels of detection may prove to be problematic if disciplinary actions are being taken in the same context as the detection in that public demonstrations of discipline are rarely, if ever, an advisable response to any unacceptable behavior.

Finally, consider the finding that suggests an apparent chasm between acknowledging the moral wrong of cheating while considering it to be socially acceptable. Although it may be tempting to shrug off the finding as even more evidence of a generation beyond moral appreciation, it is possible that the high percentages of those who acknowledge the moral wrong of academic dishonesty may be reached through discussion of ethics and brought toward the necessary reconciliation between beliefs and behaviors. And if it seems that the problem is beyond intervention, consider the response offered by Dalton (1998), who noted,

> Ethical values can be taught. Erikson (1968) believed that late adolescence was the period of life most open to ideological and ethical challenge. Youth is a time for establishing identity, and ethical commitments and values are intrinsic elements of that identity formation.... Moral development can continue into young adulthood if the circumstances in the college environment are right for promoting moral consciousness and commitment. (p. 5)

Academic Dishonesty in the Public Spotlight

In a brochure distributed by the Educational Testing Service—*The Time Has Come to Tackle Academic Cheating*—the author addressed the disintegration of the values that at one time prevented acts of academic dishonesty from happening, stating,

> As Americans enter the next millennium, many are troubled by what they see as a breakdown in traditional societal norms…. While integrity and personal pride are thought to have been key attributes of people's lives during the birth of our nation, many feel today's world is characterized by cheating—at all levels, of all sorts, all around. (Spiegel, 1999, p. 1)

Furthermore, she added,

> • Most Americans perceive cheating as widespread. Students believe that cheating is prevalent and accepted, and many believe their parents don't care or even want to know if they cheat.
> • Previously, those who cheated in school were the struggling students. Today, they are joined by above-average, college-bound students who want to ensure acceptance at elite universities.
> • On most campuses, more than 75% of students admit to some cheating. In surveys conducted in 1990, 1992, and 1995, almost 7,000 students on small- to medium-sized campuses—nearly 80 percent of undergraduate students—reported one or more incidents of cheating. (p. 1)

The prevalence of academic dishonesty has also not escaped the attention of the media. Niels (1996) confirmed that "in recent years, studies have indicated that there is an alarming increase in cheating behavior among students" (p. 5) and suggested that "in the past, it would have been easy to dismiss these reports as isolated or to look with condescension on a school which had permitted cheating to get so out of control, but not anymore. Newspaper headlines attest to the extensiveness of the problem" (p. 5). He cited the following examples:

- "Cheating by Police Alleged on Police Exams" (*Boston Globe*, April 22, 1989)
- "Plagiarism Is Rampant, A Survey Finds" (*New York Times*, April 1, 1990)
- "Cheating Shocks Pop Warner Nationally" (*Boston Globe*, October 28, 1990)
- "Cheating Isn't New, But Now It's a Way of Life" (*Los Angeles Times*, January 30, 1992)
- "Study Says Cheating Has Replaced 3R's" (*Chicago Tribune*, November 13, 1992)
- "4 of 5 Students Admit Cheating" (*Ft. Lauderdale Sun-Sentinel*, October 23, 1993)
- "Rise in Cheating Called Response to Fall in Values" (*USA Today*, August 2, 1995)
- "Students Make the Grade When Subject Is Cheating" (*Detroit News*, January 23, 1996)

According to one of the articles, the findings of student surveys on academic dishonesty revealed that plagiarism occurs far more frequently than may have been suspected. The results "showed that 91.2 percent of the students said that they had plagiarized their class work" ("Plaigarism Is Rampant," 1990, p. 36). Perhaps more astounding than the findings themselves were the students' comments on the findings:

Few students were taken aback by the study. Christine Humphrey, a senior political science major from Poland, was not surprised. "Not when I walk into a test and see so many people cheating," Miss Humphrey said. "That's how they got through high school and that's how they'll get through college." (p. 37)

Similarly, Clarke-Pearson (2001), reporting for the *Daily Pennsylvanian*, cited McCabe's (1999) finding that "more than 75 percent of college students admit to some form of cheating. About one-third of the 2,100 participating students admitted to serious test cheating, and half admitted to one or more instances of serious cheating on written assignments" (p. 1). Clarke-Pearson noted that "the pattern for high school students, the next generation of college-goers, is disturbingly similar" (p. 1), adding,

Eighty-four percent of the students surveyed last year by Who's Who Among American High School Students said that cheating was common among their high-achieving peers. Moreover, studies conducted by the Josephson Institute of Ethics show that the percentage of students who admitted to cheating on a test has risen from 61% in 1992 to 71% in 2000. (p. 1)

McCabe's study also caught the eye of the *Los Angeles Times*, which paid no small amount of attention to academic dishonesty in a series of articles in the spring of 2000. Weiss (2000) noted that "nationwide, most forms of cheating remain at or near record levels," but added that "while nearly 88 percent of faculty reported that they observed some form of serious cheating....32 percent never did anything about it" (p. 3). More recently, McCabe et al. (2001) stated that surveys of cheating among college students suggest that academic dishonesty is both prevalent and growing. But researchers of McCabe's prominence have not been the only ones to notice. Others, with a purposefully narrow scope of interest, such as Moffatt (1990), himself a professor, have added their observations and cautionary remarks regarding the prevalence of dishonesty in academe.

In a survey of 232 students at Rutgers University, only 22% stated that they had never cheated in college. The remainder was divided among those who "cheated occasionally in one or two courses" and those whose habit was more persistent. He noted,

A little under half, 45 percent, indicated that they had cheated occasionally... and the remaining third, exactly 33 percent, admitted to what might be called "hard core cheating." These heavy cheaters had cheated in an average of eight courses each during their college careers to date, with a range from "three or four" to 25 courses. Most of them had done this in the big anonymous classrooms, which are the pedagogical bread and butter of large public universities such as Rutgers—but not all. (Moffatt, 1990, p. 2)

As startling as these findings might be, Moffatt described the sample as "reasonably representative," adding,

Each year, about a third of the students in the course wrote on cheating. Perhaps nine in ten described themselves as cheaters, either occasional or regular; the remaining tenth reported on widespread cheating among their friends and acquaintances. The questionnaire was an attempt to tap the levels of cheating among the other two-thirds of the students in the class as well. (p. 2)

Describing the sample, Moffatt also noted,

When I checked the composition of the same class in an earlier year, it was disproportionately upperclassmen and women, and had a less-than-average number of science majors in it. Otherwise, it was reasonably representative of the larger student body at Rutgers in terms of undergraduate colleges belonged to, distributions of majors, grade point averages, and fraternity and sorority memberships.... There's a chance, on the other hand, that the questionnaire underestimated the levels of cheating among students enrolled in the class, for on the day it was given out, about one-third of them weren't attending. And as the information below will indicate, nonattenders are more likely to be cheaters than the diligent students who make class. (p. 2)

Why Academic Integrity Matters

Several researchers have confirmed the destructive nature of academic dishonesty, noting the peril in which it places all institutions of higher education. According to Burnett, Rudolph, and Clifford (1998),

There is a problem festering within our institutions of higher education that threatens to weaken their very foundation. The problem is more threatening than faculty–administration disputes; more costly than the recent and pervasive funding cutbacks; and has a greater potential of eroding the core of the teaching–learning process than under-prepared students or overpopulated classrooms. The problem is academic dishonesty, and the need to address the problem is paramount. (p. vii)

Similarly, Kibler (1998) addressed the detrimental effect of academic dishonesty, citing the works of others (e.g., Rafetto, 1985) who have also tried to remind us that "universities and colleges, regardless of their constitution, are responsible for providing an environment conducive to learning and excellence" (p. 23). Further on this point, he stated that the questions and challenges raised by recent reports on higher education call the institution into crisis for not fulfilling its most fundamental purposes and concluded that "reports of academic dishonesty and cheating contribute to the erosion of confidence and public support" (Kibler, 1998, p. 26). More specifically, he added, that "academic dishonesty presents a serious threat to maintaining an educationally purposeful community by undermining the foundation of an institution's integrity" and concluded that "the failure to provide and enforce adequate penalties in effect communicates approval to students, especially those who enter college with cheating patterns already in place" (p. 26).

Others have also noted the mission-critical nature of establishing cultures of academic integrity in higher education, but all have addressed higher education in general; none have addressed community colleges specifically. Dalton (1998) confirmed that academic integrity is the "quintessential moral virtue in the academic community" (p. 1) and noted that the public concern about the character building influence of higher education is greater now than in many decades. Furthermore, referring to findings of a study by the Wingspread Group on Higher Education (1993), Dalton noted the mandate for reform that characterized the study, pointing to a recommendation that "more attention [be given] to the place of values in the education of college students and the management of higher education" (p. 3). More specifically, he observed that many colleges address the concern about values through their curriculum, adding, "Cheating should not be accepted as an inevitability among college students. Instead, we must examine the nature of our efforts in higher education to teach values related to academic integrity and to actively promote ethical conduct" (p. 5). To those in positions of authority or influence, he also noted that one of the primary tasks of leadership in higher education is to create an ethical climate in which academic integrity is actively promoted and supported.

Aaron and Georgia (1994) also noted the organizational obligation of institutions of higher education to effectively address academic dishonesty:

Although faculty must be the front line, the entire institutional community—administration, faculty, and students—has a major stake in academic integrity. As Sabloff and Yeager (1989, p. 29) noted, "Academic integrity procedures enforce respect for the community, the ideals of the institution, and the consideration of peers and colleagues." Unchecked acts of academic dishonesty injure the reputation of an institution, hurt students who earn grades through honest efforts, and render unlikely any positive learning on the part of offenders. Such acts also hurt faculty since they challenge the ethics and integrity of the classroom. It is the joint responsibility of all constituencies within the collegiate community to establish, publicize, and enforce academic integrity standards. Only through such a common effort can the desired level of academic integrity be achieved. (p. 90)

Eight Reasons for Academic Concern

Whitley and Keith-Spiegel (2002) have cited the research of a variety of authors whose work has proved to be fundamental to the discussion of integrity. In *Academic Dishonesty: An Educator's Guide*, they outlined eight reasons for concern—all of which are as relevant to community college students, faculty members, and administrators as they may be to their colleagues within 4-year institutions of higher education. They are summarized here as follows.

Equity. Students who cheat may be getting higher grades than they deserve. According to a survey of high school teachers, 58% believed that cheating is partly responsible for grade inflation (Bushweller, 1999). In addition, when grades are assigned on the basis of the average score in the class or other norm-referenced means, students who do not cheat may get lower grades than they deserve because cheaters raise the class average. Teachers have an essential ethical responsibility to treat their students fairly (Keith-Spiegel, Wittig, Perkins, Balogh, & Whitley, 1993); failure to deal with academic dishonesty is a violation of this ethical obligation. Both instructors and students view a college teacher's ignoring evidence of academic dishonesty as a severe ethical violation (Morgan, Korschgen, & Gardner, 1996; Tabachnick, Keith-Spiegel, & Pope, 1991).

Character development. The moral and ethical development of students is an important mission of higher education (e.g., Dalton, 1985; Kibler, 1993; Kibler, Nuss, Peterson, & Pavela, 1988). That mission has been endorsed by the U.S. legal system in its decisions on legal challenges to institutional disciplinary actions in cases of academic dishonesty (Kibler et al., 1988). Although many faculty members, especially those at research-oriented universities, no longer see character or moral development as a part of their calling (e.g., Sandeen, 1985), faculty responses to academic dishonesty can strongly influence students' personal development. When students see other students cheating and do not see faculty members and administrators addressing such behavior, they may decide that academic dishonesty is acceptable or at least permissible. Conversely, a normative context that eschews academic dishonesty, such as the existence of an honor system, tends to discourage this behavior (McCabe & Klebe Treviño, 1993; McCabe et al., 1999).

The mission to transfer knowledge. Items central to the missions of every institution of higher education are (a) the preservation and search for knowledge; (b) the transmission of that knowledge to a new generation of citizens and scholars; and (c) the personal, social, cultural, and intellectual development of the members of the college or university community. Students who cheat their way through the higher education system do not acquire the knowledge to which their degrees are supposed to attest nor do they engage in the intellectual and moral struggles that foster personal development (Gehring & Pavela, 1994). Toleration of academic dishonesty, therefore, diminishes the intellectual and moral capital required by society for its common development and progress.

Students' morale. When honest students see some of their peers cheat and get away with it, especially if it appears that instructors do not seem to care, those students become frustrated and angry (e.g., Jendrek, 1992). Seeing other students gain the same rewards for cheating as they do for applying effort may lead them to become disenchanted and cynical about higher education. Those negative emotions may, in turn, lower honest students' motivation to learn. Some students may abandon effort as a success strategy and come to view cheating as the only way to keep up with everyone else.

Faculty's morale. Faculty members who learn that students have cheated in their classes often feel personally violated and mistreated by their students, reacting with feelings of anger and distrust (e.g., Jendrek, 1989; Johnston, 1996). Instructors also describe dealing with cheating as one of the most stressful aspects of their jobs (Keith-Spiegel, Tabachnick, Whitley, & Washburn, 1998). The negative emotions can be compounded by perceptions that administrators do not support the instructors' efforts to control academic dishonesty and to punish cheaters (e.g., Schneider, 1999; Wilson, 1998). Over time, such emotions can result in cynical attitudes toward students, administrators, and the educational process (e.g., Schneider, 1999).

Students' future behavior. Students who cheat in college frequently frequently go on to cheat in graduate and professional school and to engage in unethical business practices (e.g., Baldwin, Daugherty, Rowley, & Schwartz, 1996; Sims, 1993). Because having successfully cheated at the undergraduate and graduate levels can make it easier to cheat in one's professional career, failure to deal adequately with academic dishonesty and to educate students about the consequences of their behavior constitutes a disservice not only to the academic community, but also to society in general. In contrast, students who have been held to high academic ethics standards as undergraduates are less likely to commit ethical violations in the workplace (McCabe et al., 1996).

Reputation of the institution. Incidents of academic dishonesty, especially when they involve the collaboration of many students (e.g., a "cheating ring") or an odd feature (e.g., a student's attempt to blackmail an instructor unless copies of upcoming examinations were supplied) are of interest to the media. Having the name of the institution prominently linked with the dishonest activity can sully, at least temporarily, the institution's reputation. Should an institution experience frequent, publicized incidents of academic dishonesty, its reputation may be more permanently tarnished.

Public confidence in higher education. The effects of failing to address academic dishonesty contribute to a broader problem: the public's growing lack of confidence in the academy. Such loss of faith can easily lead to loss of support for higher education.

CHAPTER THREE

Perceptions of Students and Faculty

Introduction

Before it is possible to champion academic integrity within community colleges, it is crucial that we take an "integrity pulse," that is, that we have a basic understanding of the attitudes, beliefs, and behaviors of community college students and faculty. The data presented in this chapter for that purpose, provided by CAI founder Don McCabe, are from survey instruments designed at CAI in 2003, one for students and another for faculty. Among the institutions using the instrument were seven community colleges, yielding responses from 3,225 students and 657 faculty members. Although the sample size is relatively small compared with those in other studies of academic integrity, these data provide a much-needed starting point for examining academic integrity specifically in community colleges.

How Students Perceive the Academic Environment

Students were asked to rate the academic environment on their campuses on several factors (on a 5-point scale from *very low* to *very high*). The following percentages of students gave ratings of *high* or *very high* on those factors:

1. Severity of penalties for cheating: 67%
2. Students' understanding of policies about cheating: 52%
3. Faculty members' understanding of policies about cheating: 80%
4. Student support of policies: 48%
5. Faculty support of policies: 75%
6. Effectiveness of policies: 60%

The percentages for faculty understanding and support of policies suggest that community college students do not underestimate the values of many community college faculty members. Specifically, a clear majority (75%) of students perceived faculty support for academic integrity policies to be either *high* (40%) or *very high* (35%)—perhaps higher than it actually is. An even greater percentage (80%) indicated that faculty understanding of the policies is either *high* (40%) or *very high* (40%). Additionally, the data would suggest that community colleges (or at least individual faculty members) have responded to the issue of cheating with some system of applying penalties for cheating, because almost 7 out of every 10 students (67%) indicated the severity of penalties for cheating to be either *high* or *very high*.

To be fair, however, an analysis of the percentages of students giving a *medium* rating to these questions suggests that some were more reserved in their perceptions of their campuses. Specifically, the following percentages of students gave their campuses a *medium* rating on the same six factors:

1. Severity of penalties for cheating: 26%
2. Student understanding of policies: 31%
3. Faculty understanding of policies: 17%
4. Student support of policies: 39%
5. Faculty support of policies: 20%
6. Effectiveness of policies: 30%

Sources and Awareness of Integrity Policies

More than 8 out of 10 students (84%) reported that they had been informed about the academic integrity policies on their campuses. When asked where and how much they learned, the majority of the students indicated that they had *learned a lot* from faculty (53%). In fact, no other source came close, including the student handbook (30%), advisors (23%), first-year orientation programs (17%), and other students (12%). This response may come as a surprise to more than one community college advisor—especially given the long-held belief that students all but ignore the bureaucratized language of most college catalogs in favor of human interaction. If one looks at the same question by category— rather than by how much was learned—a similar picture comes into focus, with no particular entity appearing to match the effect of the faculty. The student handbook (38%), first-year orientation programs (33%), other students (30%), advisors (29%), faculty (28%), and even administrators (20%) rank as sources from which students only *learned some*. Interestingly, the student handbook was ranked second highest to faculty again.

Looking at the responses to determine the sources of learning when only *learned little* was reported produced a predictable result: administrators (52%) topped the list, with other students and the campus Web site (each at 43%) tying for second place. Other sources from which students *learned little* included the following: advisors (32%), first-year orientation programs (26%), and the student handbook (19%). This order of use is certainly intriguing, because it challenges what might have been believed about the technological preferences of many of the students surveyed. However, it may be the result of more diversity in ages and educational levels, which is so typically seen among community college students. Additionally, the relatively dispersed nature of their responses may suggest that community college students absorb information about academic dishonesty in much the same way they function in and out of the classroom: They browse from various sources, depending on what is most relevant, accessible, or convenient.

Discussion of Policies by Instructors

When asked to indicate how often (on a 5-point scale from *never* to *very often*) their instructors discussed policies concerning academic integrity, students responded in percentages that warrant some optimism. The following percentages of students ranked discussion of the specific policies as occurring *often* or *very often*, compared with *never*, *very seldom*, or *seldom* (in parentheses):

1. Plagiarism: 55% (45%)
2. Group work: 47% (53%)
3. Attribution of written sources: 61% (39%)
4. Attribution of Internet sources: 58% (41%)
5. Falsification of lab data: 39% (62%)
6. Falsification of research data: 44% (57%)

For three of the six policies (1, 3, and 4), the majority of students indicated higher levels of discussion; responses for #2, discussion for group work, were nearly even. The policies indicated as receiving the least discussion were fabrication or falsification of lab or research data. These lower percentages are not surprising, given that relatively few community college students engage in lab studies or research. What is most remarkable about these findings is that percentages for policies not related to lab work or research appear to indicate that community college faculty members are surpassing their colleagues in 4-year colleges and universities in how often they discuss issues relevant to academic integrity, and in percentages that are significantly higher than those shown by researchers. Researchers have suggested that fewer than 10% of undergraduate faculty members routinely discuss academic integrity with their students (Gehring, Nuss, & Pavela, 1986; Kibler et al., 1988; Nuss, 1984; Peterson, 1988).

An examination of the range of percentages for individual *never* responses serves to further emphasize that difference. For the first four policies, percentages ranged from 6% to 9%; the percentages pertaining to discussion of lab and research data falsification were 21% and 17%, respectively. Thus, the policy receiving the highest percentage of *never* responses alone at 21% pertains to lab data policies, which may be the least pertinent to community college students.

Frequency of Cheating

When asked to indicate their perception of the frequency of academic dishonesty on their campuses, community college students again appeared to believe that it is not as common as the research would suggest. The following percentages of students reported that they believed cheating to occur *never*, *very seldom*, or *seldom* in three contexts:

1. Plagiarism on written assignments: 74%
2. Inappropriate sharing in groups: 66%
3. Cheating during tests: 80%

These responses present an interesting conundrum: Students may be aware of academic dishonesty (based on the frequency of discussions reported earlier) but relatively unaware of how often it occurs in their own learning e nvironment. Similarly, and perhaps incredibly, community college students reported having observed relatively few acts of academic dishonesty, with 57% reporting that they had never seen another student cheat during tests. This result is especially compelling in light of the research results of Smyth and Davis (2003) who, in a similar survey, found that "more than 82% of the students [had] seen cheating, leaving roughly 18% who have never observed cheating" (p. 8). Any number of explanations may illuminate this result, but virtually no way exists to know whether the result is an indication of awareness, vigilance, ignorance, indifference, or the surreptitious nature of cheating itself.

Frequency and Seriousness of Specific Behaviors

Students were presented with 19 specific behaviors associated with cheating and were asked to self-report on two separate lines of questioning: (a) how often they may have engaged in the stated behavior and (b) how serious they considered the behavior to be. The responses revealed high percentages of students who indicated that they had never engaged in any of the behaviors and relatively high percentages who qualified those behaviors as *serious* (see Table 3.1). Specifically, percentages of students responding *never* to engaging in the 19 behaviors ranged from 81% to 88% for 10 of the behaviors, 71% to 79% for 6 behaviors, and 60% to 65% for 3 behaviors. These results present a contradiction of sorts, especially when juxtaposed with the research presented in previous chapters. Specifically, the percentages self-reported by the students present a strikingly different mindset than that indicated by overwhelming evidence that academic dishonesty is prevalent throughout higher education.

The percentages of students considering the behaviors to be serious forms of cheating were not quite as high but still considerably higher than the individual percentages reporting behaviors as less serious forms of cheating (i.e., *moderate* or *trivial*). Specifically, percentages of students indicating that the 19 behaviors constituted *serious* cheating ranged from 60% to 69% for 6 of the behaviors, 53% to 59% for 3 behaviors, and 41% to 49% for 4 behaviors. The percentages appear to indicate that students perceive cheating behaviors as relatively serious—a perception atypical of what might have been anticipated of students and more commonly seen among faculty members. Are community college students inherently more honest, as previously suggested by Lumsden and Arvidson (2001), or are they simply stealthier in their ability to respond with the level of political correctness that they may perceive is appropriate?

When asked to place certain acts of cheating on a continuum of trivial to moderate to serious, the data suggest that many students still do not understand what constitutes cheating. In fact, the results set forth in Table 3.1 would suggest a sort of "moral parsing" whereby honesty and dishonesty form not a dichotomy, but a continuum in itself. For example, 23% of the respondents indicated that working on an assignment with others when the instructor asked for individual work was not cheating, and another 37% indicated that it was trivial cheating. Taken together, this means that 60% of students failed to acknowledge the inherent principle of defying instructions given by an instructor for how a student should incorporate integrity into class assignments. Similarly, 52% of students considered receiving unpermitted help on assignments to be either not cheating or trivial cheating.

Table 3.1

Student Ratings of the Frequency and Seriousness of Cheating Behaviors

Behavior	Frequency of Behavior			Seriousness of Behavior			
	Never	Once	More than once	Not cheating	Trivial	Moderate	Serious
1 Fabricating or falsifying a bibliography	79%	6%	2%	14%	23%	30%	34%
2 Working on an assignment with others when the instructor asked for individual work	60%	16%	17%	23%	37%	26%	15%
3 Getting questions and answers from someone who has already taken a test	71%	14%	11%	14%	18%	26%	42%
4 In a course requiring computer work, copying a friend's work rather than doing personal work	74%	5%	3%	13%	11%	28%	49%
5 Helping someone else cheat on a test	83%	8%	4%	11%	6%	19%	64%
6 Fabricating or falsifying lab data	77%	4%	2%	14%	16%	30%	41%
7 Fabricating or falsifying research data	79%	4%	1%	11%	15%	30%	45%
8 Copying from another student during a test or exam with his or her knowledge	85%	7%	5%	11%	6%	18%	65%
9 Copying from another student during a test or exam without his or her knowledge	85%	7%	4%	11%	5%	15%	69%
10 Receiving unpermitted help on assignments	73%	12%	9%	23%	29%	28%	21%
11 Copying a few sentences from a written source without footnoting them	61%	19%	15%	16%	31%	29%	25%
12 Turning in a paper obtained from a term paper mill or Web site	87%	4%	2%	13%	9%	20%	57%
13 Copying a few sentences from the Internet without citing source	65%	16%	13%	16%	28%	29%	28%
14 Using unpermitted notes during a test	85%	6%	3%	11%	9%	22%	59%
15 Copying written material closely and turning in as original work	84%	7%	4%	11%	7%	19%	63%
16 Turning in a paper copied from another student	86%	6%	3%	11%	10%	25%	53%
17 Using a false excuse to obtain an extension	81%	9%	5%	16%	22%	27%	30%
18 Turning in work done by someone else	88%	5%	3%	11%	10%	19%	60%
19 Cheating on a test in any other way	86%	5%	3%	10%	7%	21%	62%

Note. NA responses for frequency are not included on the table.

Likelihood of Reporting Cheating

Students were asked to respond, on a 4-point scale (*very unlikely* to *very likely*), about the likelihood of the following:

1. You would report an incident of cheating that you observed.
2. The typical student at your school would report such violations.
3. A student would report a close friend.

The responses suggest that community college students have mixed feelings about the act of reporting another student for cheating. On the one hand, although 70% of students thought it *very unlikely* that a student would report a close friend, only 30% and 23%, respectively, thought it *very unlikely* that they or a typical student would report cheating. On the other hand, when the percentages of students responding *very unlikely* and *unlikely* are combined, a different picture of likelihood to report cheating emerges: 68%, unlikely to report cheating; 75%, typical students unlikely to report; and 92%, students would be unlikely to report a close friend.

The question (#1) targeting individual responses to cheating yielded a higher percentage, albeit slightly, of *likely* and *very likely* responses (32%) than did the question (#2) pertaining to students' perceptions of the typical college student's response to cheating (25%). These percentages may indicate that the respondents believe that their own sense of integrity is marginally stronger than that of their peers. Of course, a number of ways exist to analyze this differential, not the least of which is the fact that it is undoubtedly easier to give oneself the benefit of the doubt in a hypothetical, character-based series of questions. But it should be noted that the students' responses do not seem to indicate that they believed that the behaviors likely for others matched their own sense of integrity, which is ironic given the similarity of their overall responses that appear to demonstrate a relatively strong sense of academic integrity.

General Attitudes About Academic Integrity

Students were asked to indicate their agreement to nine statements designed to reveal their attitudes about integrity in their institutions. A 5-point scale was supplied, from *disagree strongly* to *agree strongly*, with *not sure* as the midpoint. For purposes of the present analysis, I combined the five sets of responses into two sets as follows: (1) disagreement or uncertainty, which combines *strongly disagree*, *disagree*, and *not sure* responses, and (2) agreement,

Table 3.2

Students' General Attitudes About Academic Integrity

Statements	Disagreement/ uncertainty	Agreement
1 Cheating is a serious problem	90%	10%
2 Review process for cheating is fair	61%	39%
3 Students should be held responsible for monitoring others	74%	26%
4 Faculty members discover and report suspected cheating	61%	39%
5 Faculty regularly change tests and assignments	51%	49%
6 Amount of course work is reasonable	26%	74%
7 Difficulty of tests and assignments is appropriate	26%	74%
8 Assessments in courses are effective	32%	68%
9 Assessment helps learning	28%	73%

which combines *agree* and *strongly agree* responses. (The individual *not sure* responses are presented, however, in Table 3.10.)

As Table 3.2 shows, with responses grouped in this way, some interesting patterns emerge. First, the recombined percentages reveal two overall trends: toward disagreement or uncertainty for the statements that pertain more directly to integrity (1–5) and toward agreement for the statements that pertain more generally to the learning climate (6–9). An analysis of the individual statements receiving the highest percentages of responses reveals other interesting trends. For example, for statement 1, an overwhelming majority of students (90%) were not sure or disagreed with the idea that cheating was a serious problem on their campuses. Although not as strongly, the trend toward disagreement or uncertainty held for the majority of responses to the other four statements pertaining to integrity (statements 2–5), ranging from 51% to 74%. For statements 6–9, the statements pertaining to course work and assessment, the percentage of agreement was consistently high, at 68% to 74%.

Analysis of the results indicates that students are more unsure than they are sure about issues relevant to academic integrity, which is interesting, given that the data indicate that there is more discussion of this topic occurring between students and faculty than might have been expected. Perhaps the uncertainty is explained by the fact that when cheating is mentioned, it happens in those tentative first moments of class when syllabi and class assignments are discussed—hardly the time for an adequate give-and-take conversation between teacher and student or, for that matter, between students.

It is also interesting to note that students registered relatively strong disagreement in response to the idea that students should be held responsible for monitoring the academic integrity of other students. Among the many possible explanations for this, the simplest may be that most students do not like to be known by their peers as a goody two shoes or a snitch. For students to feel a sense of obligation to the institution, they would need to feel a corresponding sense of moral responsibility and an equally high compunction to maintain a sense of integrity. Sadly, it seems that few community colleges place a high priority on teaching students the value of honesty. Thus, it may be easier for students to think of justice as someone else's job, not theirs. Finally, this outcome may simply be the result of students' reluctance to step into what they would likely perceive as the role of the faculty members.

Although the results show overall uncertainty about faculty vigilance, with 51%–61% collectively signaling disagreement or uncertainty to statements 4 and 5, an analysis of individual responses on the 4 points of the scale on either side of the midpoint also shows a significant level of agreement. Specifically, 3% and 10%, respectively, responded *disagree strongly* or *disagree* to statement 4, compared to *agree strongly* and *agree* (9% and 31%, respectively) at the opposite end of the scale. For statement 5, the percentages were as follows: 5% and 10% for *disagree strongly* and *disagree*, respectively, compared with 12% and 36% for *agree strongly* and *agree*, respectively.

Thus, agreement on both these statements was much greater than disagreement, and the percentages of students signaling agreement versus uncertainty (i.e., those responding *not sure*) were closer in proportion: 48% unsure versus 39% agreeing for statement 4; 37% unsure versus 49% agreeing for statement 5. This degree of agreement is significant for one important reason: Students who perceive that faculty members are indifferent to the occurrence of academic dishonesty often rationalize participation in cheating, even when they may have otherwise been disinclined to do so. The fact that students perceive that faculty members take action is critical to fostering an environment where students know not only that it is unacceptable to cheat, but also that efforts of honest students will be protected with an appropriate level of watchfulness on the part of the faculty members.

Comparison of Student and Faculty Responses

Perceptions of Academic Environment

Using the same items and scale administered to students, faculty members were asked to rate the academic environment on their campuses. As Table 3.3 shows, faculty responses differed dramatically from those of students. Although variances in responses differed substantially along all dimensions, perhaps the greatest variance can be seen in the *high* and *very high* ratings given for the six factors: A consistently lower proportion of faculty than students gave high ratings. For example, 80% of students versus 44% of faculty rated faculty understanding of policies as high. This proportionate difference persisted for ratings for all of the other factors as well, from a 28-percentage-point difference for perceptions of faculty support to a 36-point difference in high ratings of effectiveness of policies.

Table 3.3

Student and Faculty Perceptions of Academic Environment

	Students	Faculty	Students	Faculty
Factors Rated	Low/very low		High/very high	
1 Severity of penalties	7%	22%	67%	32%
2 Student understanding of policies	17%	42%	52%	18%
3 Faculty understanding of policies	3%	14%	80%	44%
4 Student support of policies	14%	32%	48%	18%
5 Faculty support of policies	4%	12%	75%	47%
6 Effectiveness of policies	10%	27%	60%	24%

Several general conclusions may be drawn from these results. It appears, for example, that students may believe the faculty to be more knowledgeable than faculty members believe themselves to be (ratings of factor 3). The data also suggest that students overestimate and that faculty underestimates student support for campus policies concerning cheating (factors 4 and 5): Whereas 48% of students indicated student support of integrity policies as *high*, only 18% of faculty members rated it as *high*; 75% of students versus 47% of faculty rated faculty support of policies as *high*.

To explain what accounts for some of the differences, it may be useful to further examine individual responses. Take, for example, perceptions of severity of penalties (67% vs. 32% of students vs. faculty rating severity as *high*). Perhaps this difference occurs because the faculty would logically have a broader frame of reference and possibly stronger feelings about the need for strong punishment. That is, it might be typical, because of community college policy or common practice, for a student to receive a failing grade for having cheated. A student might well perceive that outcome as a high penalty for cheating. However, a faculty member who is aware that other institutions suspend or expel students for having violated the integrity code might characterize the same outcome as only moderately severe. One explanation for the difference between student and faculty perceptions of the effectiveness of policies (factor 6) was suggested by McCabe: "Part of the explanation for high student ratings of effectiveness may be the fact [that] they are satisfied with the status quo—i.e., less than strict enforcement of academic integrity standards—after all, they don't think a lot of these 'things' are very serious anyway" (2005, p. 1).

Policy Discussion and Sources

The survey question regarding discussion of academic integrity policies was posed differently to students and faculty. Both groups were asked to provide ratings for six contexts; however, the rating scales differed. Students were asked to rate frequency on a 5-point scale from *never* to *very often*. The scale for faculty was as follows: *do not discuss, on individual assignments, in the syllabus, start of semester,* and *other*. Table 3.4 presents student and faculty responses in a way that allows for comparison, even though the scale anchors were not identical.

Table 3.4

Discussion of Integrity Policies Reported by Students and Faculty

	Students	Faculty	Students	Faculty			
Policy	Never– seldom	Do not discuss	Often/ very often	Specific assign- ments	In syllabus	Start of semester	Other contexts
1 Plagiarism	45%	6%	55%	29%	56%	58%	12%
2 Group work	53%	7%	47%	43%	26%	37%	9%
3 Attribution of written sources	39%	8%	61%	48%	22%	26%	11%
4 Attribution of Internet sources	41%	9%	58%	46%	17%	24%	12%
5 Falsification of lab data	62%	14%	39%	28%	19%	26%	8%
6 Falsification of research data	57%	15%	44%	15%	9%	16%	3%

The highest percentages of faculty members indicated discussing policies regarding academic dishonesty in the syllabus (56%) and at the beginning of the semester (58%), and sizable percentages reported discussing policies for individual assignments. When all four discussion scale anchors are taken into account (i.e., all responses other than *do not discuss*), including those other than individual assignments, a significant level of discussion was reported by faculty. Indeed, very low percentages of faculty indicated no discussion, and the highest percentages were for falsification of research or lab data, which, as was mentioned earlier, is probably due to the fact that relatively few community college courses involve lab and research work.

The survey question regarding the sources of academic integrity policies also differed slightly for students and faculty. Both groups were provided with a list of sources. Students were asked to indicate how much they learned from the sources, whereas faculty members were asked to indicate which sources they relied on for their information. The students' responses were summarized earlier in the chapter. To facilitate comparison, Table 3.5 presents faculty responses alongside only the students' *learned a lot* responses, assuming that sources that students indicated learning a lot from can be construed as primary sources for them. It may be useful here to emphasize one salient finding presented earlier: The source from which students learned the most about integrity policies was the faculty.

Table 3.5

Sources of Information on Integrity Policies

Sources	Students Learned a lot	Faculty Primary source
Student vs. faculty orientation	17%	44%
Campus Web site	3%	8%
Student vs. faculty handbook	30%	60%
Advisor vs. department chair	23%	31%
Students	12%	NA
Faculty	53%	37%
Deans or other administrators	8%	22%
College catalog	NA	24%
Other	3%	11%

Frequency of Cheating

A 5-point scale was provided for ratings of three factors targeting frequency of cheating: *never, very seldom, seldom, often,* and *very often.* For purposes of analysis, I combined responses into two categories, (1) never/very seldom/seldom and (2) often/very often. As Table 3.6 shows, some interesting patterns emerged. In general, a greater proportion of both students and faculty perceived cheating as occurring infrequently than as occurring often. At the same time, however, a higher percentage of students than faculty gave ratings of *seldom* to *never,* indicating a higher level of perceptions of infrequency. Conversely, more faculty than students indicated perceiving cheating as occurring often. As the data also show, however, there was relative agreement between students and faculty on both ends of the scale for one factor: cheating during tests (factor 3). Specifically, 80% of students and 74% of faculty perceived cheating on tests as occurring infrequently (*never, very seldom,* or *seldom*); 20% and 25% of students and faculty, respectively, rated cheating on tests as occurring frequently (*often* or *very often*).

An examination of individual faculty responses (not included on Table 3.6) points up some other interesting patterns. One is that faculty responses were nearly evenly divided among those rating plagiarism on assignments as occurring *seldom* (40%) and *often* (40%) and among those rating inappropriate sharing as occurring *seldom* (38%) and *often* (39%). Also of interest is that percentages of faculty members giving a rating of *never* on all three factors were almost identical, from 1% to 2%. McCabe advised that these results should not be generalized to specific conclusions, because faculty members' perceptions of frequency of cheating were included only on the most recent versions of the survey, which was administered at only two community colleges.

Table 3.6

Student and Faculty Perceptions of Frequency of Cheating

Factors Rated	Students	Faculty	Students	Faculty
	Never–seldom		Often/very often	
1 Plagiarism on written assignments	74%	49%	26%	51%
2 Inappropriate sharing in groups	66%	48%	34%	52%
3 Cheating during tests	80%	74%	20%	25%

Both students and faculty members were also asked to indicate how often they had actually observed a student cheating during a test. As Table 3.7 shows, the most significant difference between the two groups was in the percentages indicating *never*: 46% of faculty versus 57% of students. This difference is only slightly greater than it was for that reported in Table 3.6 for percentages of faculty and students perceiving cheating on tests as occurring infrequently (74% of faculty and 80% of students). There are some fairly predictable reasons why high percentages of students report having not seen cheating in action, not the least of which is the fact that in testing situations, their full attention is presumably elsewhere. High percentages of faculty members reporting witnessing cheating may be attributed to the fact that the act of evaluating written assignments, monitoring group activities, and overseeing the administration of exams all entail evaluating and ensuring that the work was the product of honest effort.

Table 3.7

Percentage of Students and Faculty Who Observed Cheating During Tests

Frequency	Students	Faculty
Never	57%	46%
Once	12%	15%
A few times	21%	30%
Several times	6%	7%
Many times	4%	2%

Frequency and Seriousness of Specific Behaviors

Faculty respondents were presented with the same 19 specific behaviors associated with cheating that students were. Whereas students were asked to indicate how often they themselves may have engaged in the stated behavior, faculty members were asked how often they may have observed students engaging in the behaviors. Student responses were summarized earlier in the chapter and in Table 3.1. In Table 3.8, student and faculty responses are compared. Highlights of the findings for the three anchors (*never, once, more than once*) are as follows:

Table 3.8

Comparison of Student and Faculty Ratings of the Frequency of Cheating Behaviors

Behavior	Never Students	Never Faculty	Once Students	Once Faculty	More Than Once Students	More Than Once Faculty
1 Fabricating or falsifying a bibliography	79%	45%	6%	4%	2%	16%
2 Working on an assignment with others when the instructor asked for individual work	60%	31%	16%	8%	17%	41%
3 Getting questions and answers from someone who has already taken a test	71%	50%	14%	7%	11%	28%
4 In a course requiring computer work, copying a friend's work rather than doing personal work	74%	25%	5%	3%	3%	11%
5 Helping someone else cheat on a test	83%	58%	8%	10%	4%	19%
6 Fabricating or falsifying lab data	77%	31%	4%	3%	2%	6%
7 Fabricating or falsifying research data	79%	29%	4%	5%	1%	11%
8 Copying from another student during a test or exam with his or her knowledge	85%	59%	7%	12%	5%	20%
9 Copying from another student during a test or exam without his or her knowledge	85%	53%	7%	13%	4%	24%
10 Receiving unpermitted help on assignments	73%	45%	4%	8%	2%	14%
11 Copying a few sentences from a written source without footnoting them	61%	22%	19%	5%	15%	46%
12 Turning in a paper obtained from a term paper mill or Web site	87%	47%	4%	8%	2%	14%
13 Copying a few sentences from the Internet without citing source	65%	26%	16%	5%	13%	42%
14 Using unpermitted notes during a test	85%	59%	6%	9%	3%	15%
15 Copying written material closely and turning in as original work	84%	32%	7%	11%	4%	34%
16 Turning in a paper copied from another student	86%	49%	6%	9%	3%	20%
17 Using a false excuse to obtain an extension	81%	42%	9%	9%	5%	30%
18 Turning in work done by someone else	88%	49%	5%	12%	3%	29%
19 Cheating on a test in any other way	86%	49%	5%	11%	3%	24%

Note. Student responses indicate frequency of engaging in the behavior. Faculty responses indicate frequency of observing the behavior. NA responses are not included on the table.

- *Never* responses show the highest differential between students and faculty: 60%–88% of students indicated never having engaged in the behaviors, whereas 22%–59% of faculty indicated never having observed the behaviors, for a 29- to 38-point difference between the two groups at the high and low ends of the scale, respectively. Looking at the percentage differences by individual behavior, the groups differed by a low of 21 points (for #3) to 52 points (for #15).
- Although less pronounced, a differential was also evident between the groups for *more than once* responses. Whereas relatively few students (1%–17%) reported having engaged in the behaviors more

than once, 6%–46% of faculty observed the behaviors more than once, for a 5- to 29-point difference between the two groups at the low and high ends of the scale, respectively. The lowest and highest percentage-point differences were 4 (for #6) and 35 (for #15).

- *Once* responses show the highest level of agreement between the groups: 4%–19% of students gave a *once* response, compared to 3%–13% for faculty. For more than half of the *once* responses, there is less than a 4-point differential between students and faculty.

The data suggest that the responses may be underestimated (by the faculty), or overestimated (by students), or a combination of both. But it remains compelling to consider the findings in the simplest terms: across the board, in reference to each of the 19 items of specific cheating behaviors, students reported never having engaged in any of the activities at rates significantly higher than faculty members report having seen them. Are those the results of savvy students responding with less candor than might be necessary to get a clear picture, or are they every bit as righteous as their responses would indicate? Are faculty members overreporting what they believe occurs, rather than what they have actually observed?

Both students and faculty members were asked to provide ratings for how serious they considered the behaviors to be. Student responses were summarized earlier in the chapter and in Table 3.1. In Table 3.9, student and faculty responses are compared. As the data on the seriousness dimension suggest, students and faculty members perceive cheating behaviors with markedly different contextual lenses. Highlights are as follows:

- The distribution of data indicates fairly distinct differences in their perceptions of the seriousness of each of the 19 cheating behaviors.
- Proportionately few faculty members indicated that any of the 19 cheating behaviors constituted either not cheating or trivial cheating.
- Proportionately more students indicated that the 19 cheating behaviors were either not cheating, trivial, or moderate.
- Those behaviors characterized as moderate cheating resulted in a wider range of results for faculty members (7%–51%) than for the students (15%–30%). The range suggests that more disagreement exists among the faculty as to what was moderate and in what proportions.

- The percentage of students acknowledging specific behaviors as serious is larger than might have been expected. However, it is not larger than the percentage of faculty members indicating the same belief.

Table 3.9

Comparison of Student and Faculty Ratings of the Seriousness of Cheating Behaviors

Behavior	Not cheating Students	Not cheating Faculty	Trivial Students	Trivial Faculty	Moderate Students	Moderate Faculty	Serious Students	Serious Faculty
1 Fabricating or falsifying a bibliography	14%	2%	23%	4%	30%	36%	34%	58%
2 Working on an assignment with others when the instructor asked for individual work	23%	2%	37%	14%	26%	51%	15%	33%
3 Getting questions and answers from someone who has already taken a test	14%	2%	18%	4%	26%	23%	42%	71%
4 In a course requiring computer work, copying a friend's work rather than doing personal work	13%	2%	11%	2%	28%	14%	49%	82%
5 Helping someone else cheat on a test	11%	1%	6%	1%	19%	11%	64%	87%
6 Fabricating or falsifying lab data	14%	1%	16%	2%	30%	20%	41%	77%
7 Fabricating or falsifying research data	11%	1%	15%	2%	30%	16%	45%	82%
8 Copying from another student during a test or exam with his or her knowledge	11%	1%	6%	1%	18%	7%	65%	92%
9 Copying from another student during a test or exam without his or her knowledge	11%	1%	5%	1%	15%	7%	69%	92%
10 Receiving unpermitted help on assignments	23%	2%	29%	11%	28%	51%	21%	36%
11 Copying a few sentences from a written source without footnoting them	16%	3%	31%	13%	29%	46%	25%	39%
12 Turning in a paper obtained from a term paper mill or Web site	13%	2%	9%	<1%	20%	7%	57%	90%
13 Copying a few sentences from the Internet without citing source	16%	2%	28%	10%	29%	46%	28%	42%
14 Using unpermitted notes during a test	11%	2%	9%	1%	22%	10%	59%	88%
15 Copying written material closely and turning in as original work	11%	1%	7%	1%	19%	11%	63%	87%
16 Turning in a paper copied from another student	11%	1%	10%	1%	25%	14%	53%	83%
17 Using a false excuse to obtain an extension	16%	3%	22%	14%	27%	39%	30%	43%
18 Turning in work done by someone else	11%	<1%	10%	2%	19%	12%	60%	85%
19 Cheating on a test in any other way	10%	2%	7%	1%	21%	13%	62%	84%

A closer look at the individual behaviors provides additional food for thought. First, it is obvious that exceptionally few faculty members considered any of the 19 cheating behaviors to be not cheating, but comparatively more community college students did. In fact, for some items, there were distinct spikes in the differences. For example, almost 1 in 4 students (23%) responded that working on an assignment with others when the instructor asked for individual work, as well as receiving unpermitted help on an assignment, was not cheating.

Second, perhaps predictably, an analysis of the trivial cheating responses did not yield results dramatically different from the responses to not cheating. What is interesting, however, is the apparent mirroring of responses between the two groups, because a comparison suggests a similarity in the response pattern (if not the degree of agreement) between the two groups. It is still apparent that far fewer faculty members perceived any act of cheating as trivial and that comparatively more students did.

Third, there is more evidence of disagreement—in both the degree to which each behavior is cheating and in the kind of cheating—in the responses to moderate cheating. In fact, this response category is unique in that it is the only category in which the faculty responses were not consistently and disproportionately lower than the student responses. Of course, the difference could mean that (a) faculty members are less inclined to categorize any cheating behavior as anything but serious or (b) at least some students are inclined to acknowledge that at least some behaviors are moderate cheating.

Last, analysis of the responses for serious cheating clearly indicates that faculty members perceived many, if not all, of the cheating behaviors as serious. However, the responses very clearly demonstrate a pattern noted earlier in that the responses of both groups, while differing in extent and extreme, mirrored each other. Perhaps that mirroring is evidence that the two groups share the same perception of the extent to which any of the behaviors are serious—they just did not agree in the same percentages.

Likelihood of Reporting Cheating

To further explore how faculty members have dealt or would deal with cheating, the faculty survey included a number of additional questions. For example, faculty members were asked "If you were convinced, even after discussion with the student, that a student had cheated on a major test or assignment in your course, what would be your most likely course of action?" The three most likely actions were as follows:

- Fail the student on the test or assignment: 58%
- Reprimand or warn student: 38%
- Redo the test or assignment: 25%

Only 1% indicated that they would take no action; less than 25% of faculty members reported the likelihood of taking other actions such as reporting the student to the chair or dean (18%, 16%), lowering the student's grade (17%), or failing the student for the course (12%).

Interestingly, although 1% indicated doing nothing as a likely course of action upon detecting cheating, when asked whether they had ever ignored a suspected incident of cheating, 32% said yes. Although many things may explain this behavior, it might be important to point out that the two things (doing nothing and ignoring an act of cheating) are not necessarily synonymous. With that said, however, it does appear, to be a contradiction in terms. There is plenty of anecdotal evidence to support the perilous nature of reporting cheating. In some instances, faculty members themselves run the risk of being unsupported, harassed, or even ordered to take a course of action in violation of their principles. In short, for some, doing nothing or ignoring an act of cheating may reflect a callous disregard for professional integrity, but for others, the situation may be infinitely more complex.

General Attitudes
Both students and faculty members were asked to indicate the extent to which they agreed or disagreed with nine statements about integrity in their institutions. Student responses were summarized earlier and in Table 3.2. In Table 3.10, I present a comparison of their responses. As with Table 3.2., for purposes of analysis, I combined the five sets of responses into two sets as follows: (1) disagreement or uncertainty, which combines *strongly disagree*, *disagree*, and *not sure* responses and (2) agreement, which combines *agree* and *strongly agree* responses. Because the *not sure* responses signal a high level of agreement for the five statements that both groups provided responses for, they are also included in Table 3.10. Note in particular the level of agreement for statements 1–3.

The high level of agreement between the groups on those statements is interesting in itself, but also in relation to the two ends of the scale. As has been the case in previous response analyses, a familiar pattern is apparent in that reverse trends exist on both sides for the two groups. For example, whereas students and faculty were nearly equally unsure whether cheating was a serious problem, a higher percentage of students (90%) than faculty (68%) indicated disagreement/uncertainty; conversely, a significantly higher percentage of faculty (32%) versus students (10%) indicated agreement (see Table 3.10). This reverse trend persists for statements 2 and 3 as well: 61% of students versus 46% of faculty indicated disagreement/uncertainty; 54% of faculty versus 39% of students indicated agreement (statement 2). For statement 3, 74% of students versus 55% of faculty indicated disagreement/uncertainty; 45% of faculty versus 26% of students indicated agreement.

Table 3.10

Comparison of General Attitudes of Students and Faculty About Academic Integrity

Statement	Students	Faculty	Students	Faculty	Students	Faculty
	Disagreement/ uncertainty		*Not sure* responses alone		Agreement	
1 Cheating is a serious problem	90%	68%	45%	47%	10%	32%
2 Review process for cheating is fair	61%	46%	49%	49%	39%	54%
3 Students should be held responsible for monitoring others	74%	55%	25%	25%	26%	45%
4 Faculty members discover and report suspected cheating	61%	NA	48%	NA	39%	NA
5 Faculty regularly change tests and assignments	51%	NA	37%	NA	49%	NA
6 Amount of course work is reasonable	26%	NA	13%	NA	74%	NA
7 Difficulty of tests and assignments is appropriate	26%	NA	15%	NA	74%	NA
8 Assessments in courses are effective	32%	8%	19%	19%	68%	92%
9 Assessment helps learning	28%	8%	15%	15%	73%	93%

Note. Percentages may not add to 100 due to rounding. *Not sure* percentages are included in the percentages shown for disagreement/uncertainty.

It is reasonable to suggest that the difference in responses to statement 1 and in other responses is a reflection not simply of agreement or disagreement, but of perspective and investment. Of course, faculty members perceive cheating to be serious when they observe it in the proportions this group has reported. Students who report the levels of never having cheated would also report that they disagree with the statement that cheating might be a serious problem at their colleges. However, because faculty members often understand academic dishonesty as being more than disparate acts of dishonesty (as may be the students' perspective), they are also proportionately more likely to perceive it as a more serious threat—not just to their college, but to their lifestyle, their moral codes, and their entire value system—none of which students would be expected to reference in order to respond to this question.

The reasoning behind students' responses to statement 3 is not difficult to understand; students operate within a different frame of reference than do faculty members. There is little tolerance for one who is perceived by his or her peers to be a snitch or holier than thou. It is also possible that the responses originated from community college students who, at least in some large part, are nontraditional and perceive themselves as having little time for activities outside what is required for academic credit. To them, perhaps, being responsible for the moral (or immoral) behavior of others may seem little more than an irrelevant abstraction.

However, the faculty perspective is equally compelling. Aware of what mature adults know about the ongoing development of students, the faculty may perceive that students might be better suited to create a more relevant environmental press in which other students will choose honesty over dishonesty. Also, it is possible that the entire process of policing academic dishonesty is something that is increasingly distasteful for many who see themselves in the role of mentor, facilitator, guide, and instructor—not as one who is responsible for policing or enforcing academic integrity—no matter how much it might be valued.

Students' responses to statements 4 and 5 illuminate the extent to which students perceive the faculty as being immediately and actively involved in preventing academic dishonesty. As with statements 1–3, students appear to have applied the benefit of the doubt (seen in individual *not sure* responses). One explanation for students' uncertainty may be that they have a tendency not to notice when a student has been caught cheating, provided that the faculty member in question is familiar with the proper process for handling such situations confidentially and with as little public commotion as possible.

The issue of preventing academic dishonesty was posed differently to faculty. On the faculty survey, they were asked to indicate what safeguards they use to reduce cheating in their classes. Their responses indicate that they are quite involved in the identification, discussion, and prevention of academic dishonesty. In rank order, the safeguards used were as follows:

1. Monitor students during tests: 79%
2. Change tests regularly: 64%
3. Discuss personal views on academic integrity with students: 62%
4. Provide information about cheating and plagiarism on the syllabus: 61%

5. Use different versions of tests: 41%
6. Remind students periodically of academic integrity policies: 38%
7. Use the Internet to confirm plagiarism: 19%
8. Other: 14%
9. None: 6%

Perhaps to no one's surprise, students and faculty members appear to have different perspectives on the effectiveness of course assessment. As responses to statements 8 and 9 reveal, overall, more faculty (92% and 93%) than students (68% and 73%) indicated that assessments are effective and helpful. The primary difference between the two groups, however, lies primarily in the extent to which they agreed—that is, in the difference between *agree* and *strongly agree* responses taken individually. Specifically, *agree* responses were relatively even: 55% and 57% of students and faculty, respectively, gave *agree* responses for statement 8, compared with 13% and 35% of students and faculty, respectively, giving *agree strongly* responses. Similarly, for statement 9, the percentages of students versus faculty agreeing were 58% and 54%, respectively, and strongly agreeing, 15% and 39%, students versus faculty, respectively.

Conclusion

The data presented here suggest that community college faculty members and students have much to be proud of. Despite 50 years of research in which academic dishonesty in higher education has been typified as prevalent and epidemic, a significant number (57%) of community college students report never having seen cheating on their campuses. McCabe offered a comparative percentage of 40% for all colleges and universities. Although evidence suggests that cheating is rampant and that some colleagues at 4-year institutions are indifferent to cheating, the majority of community college faculty members report actively working to diminish the frequency of academic dishonesty.

The data presented in this chapter give cause for hope. However, because so little is known about academic dishonesty in the community college arena, it is probably not wise to extrapolate these data too far. I think it is safe to speculate that much can be learned from these data and that they provide a foundation on which to call others to action. To that end, in the next two chapters I present a number of strategies for taking action and profile meaningful actions taken by several community colleges around the country.

CHAPTER FOUR

Strategies for Promoting a Culture of Integrity

Introduction

After becoming familiar with the research related to the issue of academic dishonesty, it is easy to see some students as incorrigible perpetrators of an academic plague. Even if they deny either seeing or participating in cheating in the numbers made evident in previous chapters, it is easy to dismiss their responses as just another facet of denial, just another feeble rationalization, just another assault on the foundational values inherent to higher education. But like most traps, the entry is easier than the exit. Community college administrators and faculty can do more to encourage honest academic behavior from students. However complex the question of academic dishonesty may seem at this point, we know more now than we ever have in the past, certainly enough to marshal our energies toward both short-term action and long-term solutions. Beginning at the beginning, the single most critical step we can take is creating a culture of integrity, where honest academic behavior is expected, protected, and rewarded.

The preceding chapters have focused on defining academic dishonesty, summarizing and analyzing the research on its prevalence and the attitudes underlying it, and articulating the rationale for addressing the issue. Because one of the most effective ways to discourage academic dishonesty is to encourage academic integrity, I turn now to outlining some strategies for establishing and building a collegewide climate of academic integrity. Whitley and Keith-Spiegel (2002) referred to this climate as an "integrity ethos" that requires a common vision, leadership from the top, systemic change, and a long-term perspective. They cited institutional integrity, a learning-oriented environment, a values-based curriculum, and an honor code among the elements needed to create such an ethos. The strategies I present are drawn from my own experience and perspectives and from the work of many researchers in addition to Whitley and Keith-Spiegel (e.g., Alschuler and Blimling; Burke; Burnett, Rudolph, and Clifford; Gehring and Pavela; Kibler; McCabe and colleagues).

Readers will also find that the strategies presented here address the recommendations published by CAI (1999) in *The Fundamental Values of*

Academic Integrity, the introduction to which begins with "As this document …makes clear, academic integrity is essential to the success of our mission as educators. It also provides a foundation for responsible conduct in our students' lives after graduation" (p.1) and ends with "Raising the level of student academic integrity should be among our highest priorities on college and university campuses" (p. 2). According to CAI, to develop strong programs for promoting the values of academic integrity, academic institutions should

1. Have clear academic integrity statements, policies, and procedures that are consistently implemented.
2. Inform and educate the entire community regarding academic integrity policies and procedures.
3. Promulgate and rigorously practice these policies and procedures from the top down, and provide support to those who faithfully follow and uphold them.
4. Have a clear, accessible, and equitable system to adjudicate suspected violations of policy.
5. Develop programs to promote academic integrity among all segments of the campus community. These programs should go beyond repudiation of academic dishonesty and include discussions about the importance of academic integrity and its connection to broader ethical issues and concerns.
6. Be alert to trends in higher education and technology affecting academic integrity on its campus.
7. Regularly assess the effectiveness of its policies and procedures and take steps to improve and rejuvenate them. (CAI, 1999, p. 10)

Make Academic Integrity an Institutional Priority

Involve All Constituents
Addressing academic dishonesty and promoting integrity require the awareness, commitment, and involvement of *all* community college constituents: faculty, students, administrators, and boards of trustees. The role that faculty members play is obvious: Because they have more direct contact with students, they may be in the best position to educate students about academic dishonesty and to detect it when it occurs. What needs to be remembered in the community

college context, however, is that part-time faculty members, who constitute approximately 60% of faculty, also need be included in all integrity efforts undertaken at the college.

Burke described the collaborative role that students may play as follows:

> Since faculty members view students as primarily responsible for reducing academic dishonesty, students might be considered partners in programmatic efforts to reduce cheating and plagiarism. A cooperative venture between faculty and students might significantly [affect] academic dishonesty at the college. In colleges that have successfully addressed academic dishonesty with an Honor Code, perhaps the most vital element has not been the Honor Code itself, but the resultant discussion and collaboration between faculty and students. (1997, pp. 138–139)

But, as Whitley and Keith-Spiegel and many others have asserted, primary responsibility for making academic integrity an institutional priority resides with the college leaders. These leaders include all administrators within the college, as well as the board of trustees. Chairs, division directors, deans, chief academic and student affairs officers, presidents, chancellors, and trustees are empowered to provide coaching, moral and financial support, technical assistance, policy advice, legal access and support, and ongoing resources for activities and professional development.

Whitley and Keith-Spiegel elaborated on the importance of promoting academic integrity from the leadership level down:

> Change must have the clear support of the institutional leaders. Schein (1985) suggested that there are at least three ways in which leaders influence organizational culture. First, members of an organization are going to see as important the things to which leaders pay attention, measure, and control. For example, if the president of an institution and faculty and student governance groups request periodic reports on academic integrity issues, then members of the institution will place more importance on academic integrity than in the absence of such interest. Second, leaders' reactions to critical incidents reveal cultural values. For example, if a star athlete is caught cheating on an

exam and the president makes excuses rather than takes corrective action, the true value placed on academic integrity at that institution becomes unmistakably clear. Similarly, if faculty, administration, or staff members who commit scientific or other serious forms of misconduct are protected or dealt with superficially, commitment to integrity will be viewed as mere window dressing. Finally, leaders both consciously and (as in the last examples) unconsciously model behaviors and make policy statements that members of the institution use as a basis for their own behavior. To the extent that leaders' behavior and statements model and support academic integrity, others will follow. (2002, pp. 152–153)

It should be stressed that trustees are also in an ideal position to play a significant role in promoting academic integrity. De Russy (2003) affirmed that any campaign that addresses ethics must involve trustees, because they play a critical role within the nation's colleges and universities in fostering, developing, and defending an ethical environment for both the college and the community it serves:

[T]rustees should ... act more directly to make ethics a living tradition, a day-to-day reality, throughout higher education. They must be activists. That requires supporting the adoption of—and providing funds for—policies that foster continuing education in the tradition of ethics of higher education, and the social compact between society and the professoriate that is at its core. Executive leadership in other professions—from medicine and law to post-Enron business—is already moving in the direction of proactive education in ethics. (p. 3)

Community colleges committed to academic integrity should initiate and complete informal, research-based "integrity audits" to determine the extent to which their campus ethos effectively supports academic integrity and—with the input of students, faculty, staff, administrators, and trustees—to identify and address areas of improvement. (See Table 4.1 for some exploratory questions.)

Table 4.1

How Prepared Is Your Campus to Address Academic Dishonesty?

The following are some questions to help you begin your exploration.

- Do faculty members and administrators have the skills or tools to confront instances of academic dishonesty?

- Is academic dishonesty discussed in professional development seminars or at state or national conferences?

- Does a policy on academic dishonesty exist? A statement on academic integrity? An honor code?

- Does an adjudication process exist to mediate and resolve instances of academic dishonesty?

- Does the college's leadership encourage faculty and staff to follow the same principles of integrity that are given to students? Are faculty and staff held accountable if they do not?

- Do those responsible for student life promote the principles of academic integrity as actively as they promote, for example, a social occasion or athletic event?

- Is an academic integrity policy reflected in the college's mission or value statements? Is it included on the Web site or in marketing materials?

- Are those who exhibit academic integrity (e.g., honest students or those who report cheating) treated fairly?

- Does the college engage trustees and local, state, and national leaders in discussion of academic dishonesty?

Identify and Appoint an "Integrity Chair"

While writing this book, I reviewed the CAI roster and found that of 421 members, only 29 (15.5%) were community colleges. Dennis Johnson (personal communication, September 4, 2005), interim dean of student services at Pueblo Community College and a former CAI board member, posited one explanation for the comparatively low number of community colleges affiliated with the CAI. Most community college staff members have many jobs and are pulled in many directions. Integrity is seen as important to both the faculty and student judicial affairs officers, but their multiple duties prohibit adding one more job. Unlike community colleges, many universities have a larger staff and people designated to concentrate on such issues.

Even when academic dishonesty is acknowledged as a priority issue in community colleges, it may not receive the priority attention it merits. One reason for this is that community colleges already face a multitude of other challenges. Most face state or federal funding issues, enrollment crises, impending retirements of seasoned faculty members and leaders, and challenges to assess institutional effectiveness quantitatively and qualitatively. Another reason is that few among the existing staff are available to take on additional responsibility.

To ensure that academic integrity is made an institutional priority, every college should identify an "integrity officer" or "integrity chair." An integrity officer would lead the implementation of the strategies recommended in this chapter, which would include communicating integrity as an institutional priority and reviewing college policies (in cooperation with all constituencies) regarding academic dishonesty and recommending modifications. Perhaps the most important role of the integrity chair would be to work individually with students and student groups, faculty and faculty councils, administrators, and executive leadership to actively promote academic integrity as a part of the organizational culture. CAI offers a variety of resources that would be useful to an integrity officer (see page 106).

Make Academic Integrity a Component of Institutional Effectiveness

Increasingly, colleges have been called upon to assess the effectiveness of their institutions in general and the quality of student learning in particular. This focus on accountability has been driven, in large part, by demand from the primary and secondary consumers of higher education (students and parents and employers, respectively) and from higher education funding sources (local, state, and federal governments and agencies)—constituents who expect colleges to ensure a verifiable return on their investments. For community colleges, in particular, effectiveness measures are intended to demonstrate that the colleges are fulfilling their primary mission: student learning. (For a comprehensive summary of the effectiveness movement from a community college perspective, see Roueche, Johnson, & Roueche, 1997; for information on developing an assessment model, see Alfred, Shults, & Seybert, 2007).

What happens when constituents learn that the data on which the institutional effectiveness efforts are based are tainted by the fact that a percentage of students who are counted as successful met their learning objectives through less-than-honest effort? Given the prevalence of cheating in the nation's colleges and the emphasis on assessing student learning, what happens when assessment results show that a college has no process in place to collect, report, or analyze such data?

In its summary of the support it provides to assist institutions in assessing the climate of academic integrity on their campuses, CAI cites the following, which constitutes a sound list of recommendations for any institution seeking to incorporate its academic integrity efforts into overall institutional assessment.

- Evaluate current academic integrity programs and policies.
- Assess campus attitudes and conduct in the classroom, the lab, and the exam room.
- Identify areas—from sanctions to educational programs—that need strengthening.
- Develop specific plans for improving the adherence to standards of academic honesty.
- Give prominence on campus to a dialogue about academic integrity.
- Increase the awareness of academic integrity issues among faculty, students, and administrators. (CAI, 2007)

Develop Well-Defined and Comprehensive Policy Statements

Adopt and Modify Honor Codes and Other Documents

Every higher education institution should examine all of its policy statements and ensure that these documents address academic integrity to the degree necessary to delineate both what is necessary for compliance to institutional policy, what the consequences are for those who do not comply, and what the process for handling midconduct is for everyone involved. This examination should begin with the honor code, whether that means adopting one for the first time or modifying an existing one. Although there has been scant research on honor codes, there is evidence to suggest that

- The existence of an honor code helps communicate academic integrity as a clear institutional priority.
- Less cheating seems to occur in institutions that have honor codes.
- Honor codes that are modified to be more comprehensive may do a better job of educating students about academic integrity. Furthermore, although modified honor codes are usually developed to educate and to address academic infractions, they often mature into codes that govern social as well as academic behavior.

When 122-some students were accused of cheating on term papers at the University of Virginia (UVA) early in 2001, some other students criticized the university's long-standing honor code on the grounds that just having students sign pledges not to cheat did not prevent cheating. One student said, "The honor system at the university needs to go. Our honor system routinely rewards cheaters and punishes honesty" (cited in McCabe & Klebe Treviño, 2002). Another stated, "I think the honor system's an ideal....it sets up for people to cheat and steal and lie" (Schemo, 2001). According to McCabe and Klebe Treviño, however, honor codes do work:

> We could not disagree more ... with the idea that it's time ... to abandon the honor system. We believe instead that America's institutions of higher education need to recommit themselves to a tradition of integrity and honor. Asking students to be honest in their academic work should not fall victim to debates about cultural relativism. Certainly, such recommitment seems far superior to throwing up our hands in despair and assuming that the current generation of students has lost all sense of honor. Fostering integrity may not be an easy task, but we believe an increasing number of students and campuses are ready to meet the challenge. (2002)

McCabe and Klebe Treviño's research (of more than 14,000 students surveyed on 58 campuses over a decade) indicated that honor codes have a strong impact on college campuses, suggesting that they have an ethical appeal for students that can help reduce cheating: "The level of self-reported cheating by students on honor-code campuses, even those with unproctored exams, is significantly lower than that on campuses without codes, where exams are often carefully monitored" (2002). It could well be that the real problem at UVA was not that the honor code was irrelevant, but that it was not comprehensive enough. Timothy Dodd (2007), former executive director of CAI, recommended that the following elements be included in modified honor codes:

- Responsibility for initiating and monitoring honor codes should be shared by students, faculty, and administrators.
- Students should be represented on hearing panels and be granted majority voting rights, and they should be encouraged to play a leading role in educating peers and faculty.

- Faculty members should be empowered to adjudicate first offenses and impose sanctions according to agreed-upon guidelines while also be required to report violations to the integrity officer or other administrator charged with that duty.
- Hearing panels should be established to adjudicate subsequent offenses reported for the same student, and panels should be empowered to impose stronger sanctions for repeat offenses.
- Sanctions should be devised creatively so that they are not solely punitive but also address the nature of and motive for offenses and the academic and ethical development needs of the violator.
- A nontoleration clause should be considered (often expressed as an obligation to act or respond or a duty to care), which does not carry a sanction if not invoked.

Anyone who has ever attempted to control an issue as complex as academic dishonesty with a single college policy has learned the definition of futility. Attempting to curb every incident of cheating with an appropriate behavioral sanction is the equivalent to trying to hold the ocean back with a broom. That much said, however, there is simply no situation worse than attempting to effect justice absent a college policy (see Clos, 2002), so a few words of advice seem helpful at this juncture. An Internet search of, for example, "community college academic integrity policy" will yield hundreds of samples to consider. But the question herein is quality, not quantity, and what makes good policy varies from college to college according to its own culture.

The CAI Web site includes links to more than 50 college and university integrity policies, inluding that of Oakton Community College, which is discussed in chapter 5. Two other policies that may be particularly relevant for community colleges in addition to others featured in chapter 5 are those of Temple College (2005) and Genesee Community College (2006). (See the reference list for URLs.) In its *Students Rights and Responsibility Handbook*, Genesee includes among its policy statements one that deals specifically with plagiarism and cheating. In the Student Code of Conduct, it outlines a very comprehensive policy that covers all forms of misconduct and a process for reporting and adjudicating misconduct.

Establish a Legally Defensible Process for Reporting and Adjudication

No honor code or other single strategy for building a climate of integrity can be effective unless comprehensive policies and procedures exist for reporting and adjudicating misconduct. A well-defined process (which, ideally, is overseen by an integrity officer and has been communicated via honor code and other institutional policy statements) serves several critical purposes. It

1. Sends a clear message to all constituents that the college is serious about its commitment to academic integrity.
2. Ensures that both students and faculty are more likely to report misconduct and that their concerns are heard and respected or acted upon in a fair, consistent, and professional manner.
3. Provides a means of collecting data that can be used in reporting institutional effectiveness.
4. Helps protect colleges in the event of litigation.

Because the legal aspects of academic dishonesty are rather complicated, faculty members and administrators alike may understandably be underinformed or confused about their rights when confronted with academic dishonesty. Pavela outlined four primary recommendations as follows:

> [L]egal issues ... must be considered in developing a comprehensive program to protect academic integrity on campus. First, it will be necessary to determine if academic dishonesty is to be considered a disciplinary offense or a matter of academic judgment. Second, clear and equitable standards and procedures for resolving academic dishonesty cases will need to be developed. Third, faculty members and others responsible for reporting or resolving allegations of academic dishonesty must be advised of pertinent legal risks, including the law of defamation. Finally, considerable thought must be given to the nature of any penalty to be imposed....These legal issues can be resolved with assurance that college ... faculty members acting reasonably and in good faith have little to fear in terms of legal liability. (1988, p. 37)

Perhaps the most startling element of Pavela's advice is the necessity to determine whether acts of academic dishonesty will be considered disciplinary offenses (adjudicated by student services or student judicial officials) or academic misconduct worthy of logical academic sanctions (adjudicated by the full authority of the faculty). Tradition and an inclination to "do it the way it has always been done" may have needlessly confused many a well-meaning faculty. Historically, student development personnel have been charged with adjudicating academic dishonesty, which has typically been categorized as a behavior along with other behaviors needing disciplinary action (ranging from issues as trivial as a parking ticket to those as serious as threats of violence). But just because adjudication has typically been handled this way is the least convincing argument to justify continuing in a similar manner, especially when there is little evidence that this method is effective. Furthermore, categorizing academic dishonesty as a student behavior to be dealt with by student development personnel rather than as an *academic infraction with academic consequences* removes from the adjudication process those who should be more involved, not less: the faculty.

Consider research into the reasons why some faculty members overlook instances of misconduct. The findings suggest that teachers typically distrust the adjudication process as it occurs outside the academic function of the college; they perceive it to be a complicated and faculty-unfriendly process. But Pavela noted that "complex, trial-type cases need not be followed in academic dishonesty cases or in other cases involving student discipline" (1988, p. 42). He continued,

At many campuses across the country, disciplinary systems have become "mired in legalistic disputes over rules or evidence" (Lamont, 1979, p. 85). As a result, students are encouraged to view campus disciplinary hearings as an "intricate chess game of procedural moves and countermoves" (American Council on Education, 1983, p. 15), rather than a means to ascertain pertinent facts and to produce a just outcome. The attitudes [that] are fostered by such a process are particularly pernicious in academic dishonesty cases, [because] faculty members are understandably reluctant to pursue allegations in what may appear to be the functional equivalent of a criminal trial. As a consequence, some faculty members ignore academic dishonesty altogether, thereby putting honest students at a competitive disadvantage. Others simply lower the grades of students whom they presume guilty of cheating or plagiarism. Both practices injure students without any due process at all, and prevent identification of repeat offenders. (pp. 42–43)

To ensure that misconduct does not go ignored, the evidence suggests the need to reevaluate structure and purposeful involvement of the entire campus community—not just one portion of it. Aaron (1992) asserted that "[p]residents and academic officers must become involved if colleges and universities are to foster the needed degree of concern and cooperation among all constituent groups" (p. 113).

Bricault (1998) methodically researched and refuted another long-standing misconception: that litigation over academic dishonesty—even within appropriate parameters of policy and due process—would inevitably result in legal reversal. He observed,

> A third and final dichotomy is whether cheating and plagiarism should be treated as academic or social misconduct. This distinction has not always been clear to the courts, which view scholastic dishonesty as "an offense [that] cannot be neatly characterized as either 'academic' or 'disciplinary'" (*Jaska v. Regents of University of Michigan*, 1984, p. 1248). When the infraction is considered academic, "by and large the American courts have been loathe to involve themselves …, accepting as a general rule noninterference in a university's purely academic decisions" (Dwyer & Hecht, 1994, p. 7). (Bricault, 1998)

Bricault continued,

> [C]ourts have generally deferred to an institution's academic judgment (Dwyer & Hecht, 1994), illustrated by such landmark cases as *Woodruff v. Georgia State University* (1983), *Regents of University of Michigan v. Ewing* (1985), *Swidryk v. Saint Michael's Medical Center* (1985), and *Susan M. v. New York Law School* (1990) and upheld by more recent court decisions, such as *Blaine v. Savannah County Day School* (1997). However, if the lawsuit moves away from the academic into the disciplinary arena, the courts are more willing to intervene. Even though such lawsuits involve fundamental constitutional rights—due process, property claims, or civil rights—not all of the constitutional safeguards afforded to criminal defendants are guaranteed to the cheaters (Swem, 1987; Dwyer & Hecht, 1994), such as

the right to produce and/or cross-examine witnesses (*Reilly v. Daly*, 1996). (Bricault, 1998, p. 7)

Although the potential for litigation is real, it may not be as prevalent as many faculty and administrators may fear. For faculty members (who are usually in the best position to detect academic dishonesty), the high-profile court cases and media attention that can result from academic misconduct can be a powerful deterrent to confronting the academic dishonesty that occurs in their own class-rooms—especially when no process exists to guide them. What many faculty members and administrators may not realize, however, is that most court cases involving academic misconduct revolve around the *manner* of adjudication, not the mere fact of it. For the most part, federal and state courts consider adjudication of plagiarism or cheating by students to be the jurisdiction of the college. Courts will rarely get involved in academic dishonesty disputes unless the accused's due process or civil rights are at issue in the college's handling of the matter. Thus, the importance of having a strong adjudication process is to ensure that misconduct is handled in such a manner that students are afforded due process that protects their constitutional rights.

Incorporate Ethics Into the Curriculum

Whereas establishing an honor code is perhaps the best way to incorporate ethics into institutional policy, the best way of communicating and reinforcing the principles set forth in a college's honor code may be to ensure that the same principles are evident in the curriculum. Whitley and Keith-Spiegel (2002) and others have asserted that ethics should be incorporated into the college curricula, not only because higher education has an obligation to attend to students' character development as well as learning, but also because ethics education is key to maintaining a climate of integrity.

[A]cademic integrity is most effectively fostered in an academic environment that encourages ... overall moral development.... Because ethical thinking, like other aspects of critical thinking, is best developed through practice, institutions should make ethical decision making a central part of their curricula. For example, institutions could require an ethics course as a part of their core curricula, require all courses to include discussions of the ethical issues relevant to the course topic, or make a departmental course in professional ethics a graduation requirement. … In addition, the institution could sponsor speakers on ethical issues and encourage departmental colloquia on ethics by offering supplemental funding for them. Examples of such institution-wide programs are published annually in the John Templeton Foundation's Honor Roll for Character-Building Colleges (e.g., John Templeton Foundation, 1997). (Whitley & Keith-Spiegel, 2002, p. 151)

Furthermore, evidence suggests that colleges can do much to offset the "anything goes" mind-set so often identified in the research as contributing to academic dishonesty:

For many students, college is the primary gateway to the "good life" of material rewards and status … the pressure on students to do well academically has seldom been greater and creates a milieu in which students often feel compelled to achieve good grades by whatever means necessary.…The traditional social prohibitions against cheating appear to have weakened in their influence on college students. Although it is difficult to measure the changing influence of family, religious institutions, and other character-building institutions on today's youth in any objective way, there is considerable concern by educators that today's students come to college with less ethical training and guidance. The combination of increased academic competition, condoning peer culture, and weakened character education makes today's college students more susceptible to the problem of academic dishonesty. (Dalton, 1998, pp. 2–3)

Whitley and Keith-Spiegel outlined several strategies for incorporating ethics into the curriculum, strategies that have been suggested by others as well. Interestingly, these strategies are identical to those suggested for creating more civil campus climates (see Rookstool, 2007). Indeed, plagiarism and cheating may be seen as acts of incivility.

- Offer a full course in ethics (perhaps even as part of the core curriculum, as a graduation requirement.

- Embed discussion of ethics in existing curricula.
- Incorporate special ethics-related activities into courses.
- Organize seminars, workshops, and other special programs for the benefit of the entire campus.

In the introduction to *The Templeton Guide: Colleges That Encourage Character Development*, a book that profiles exemplary colleges participating in the College and Character Initiative, Templeton and Schwartz (1999) addressed the need for character development during the college years:

A great many college students strive to live lives of good character. They are honest and hard working, and they care deeply about those less fortunate. Other students do not yet show consistent patterns of good character, but nonetheless they are searching for the kind of person they want to become. Recognizing this, college educators play an important role in reinforcing and strengthening the ideals and moral values that students already hold. They provide and encourage meaningful opportunities for college students to learn about, reflect on, and practice the virtues of personal and civic responsibility.... Ernest Boyer eloquently captured the belief that at the very heart of higher education is not the cultivation of skills or the learning of certain branches of knowledge, but the formation of good character. (p. 2)

Employ New Strategies for Detecting and Discouraging Technology-Aided Cheating

Understand the Impact of Generational Differences
Today's traditionally aged college students, often referred to as echo boomers, Generation Y, or millennials, are the first generation to come of age with a fully developed technological infrastructure that has wrought enormous changes over the past 20 years. The offspring of the original baby boomers, most of whom were not exposed to the newest technology until middle age, are different from their predecessors in several important ways: "They are the first to grow up with computers at home, in a 500-channel TV universe. They are multi-taskers with cell phones, music downloads, and Instant Messaging....They are totally plugged-in citizens of a worldwide community" (Kroft, 2005).

As was stated earlier, many millennials have different notions than do other generations about what constitutes moral behavior (Josephson Institute of Ethics, 2004), a finding supported by Howe and Strauss, who have studied extensively the differences in the values, perspectives, and behaviors of the different generations within a historical context (see Howe & Strauss, 2000, 2003; Strauss & Howe, 1991, 1997). Howe and Strauss have described millennials as not being able to make clear distinctions between "traditional notions of exam 'cheating' and modern notions of information 'morphing'" (2003, p. 120). Wotring summarized the underlying cause posited by Howe and Strauss as follows:

> For a number of reasons, during the 1990s, "schools prepared Millennials to be outer-driven, ideal-following team players" (Howe & Strauss, 2000, p. 166), but academic honesty was not one of the ideals widely promoted. Stemming from both their socialization to a high degreee of team orientation and the intense pressure that many feel for academic success, Millennial students are predicted to have difficulty recognizing traditional operational definitions of academic honesty (Howe & Strauss, 2003). (Wotring, 2007)

Summing up the institutional importance of understanding generational differences, Wotring (2007) stated,

> As community colleges find student Baby Boomers, Gen Xers, and Millennials sitting in the same classrooms and seeking the same support services, we all—faculty, staff, and administrators— must understand the generational differences among these students in order to best serve them all. According to the forces and perspectives described by Howe and Strauss, what is labeled as "cheating" by a Baby Boomer may well be labeled "team-work" by a Millennial. An understanding of these differences is essential to fulfillment of the academic mission to promote integrity.

More specifically, however, a better understanding of the millennial student helps explain why technology-aided cheating has become such a problem, particularly that involving use of the Internet. Millennials have grown up in an era in which Ethernet cards have replaced encyclopedias, Web sites and wireless networks have replaced the need for a clandestine cache of term papers, and an ever-increasing obsession with expediency has replaced traditional scholarly effort. Thus, in essence, they have greater access to information but less understanding of how to use it responsibly. And, as McCabe (2005) observed, there is good reason to believe that much of the problem of academic dishonesty involves use of the Internet, which is why Internet plagiarism dominates discussions of detecting and preventing cheating.

Know the Technology and Establish Guidelines for Its Use

Today's students have access to all manner of electronic devices, including laptops, PDAs, cell phones, pagers, iPods, and MP3 players. Through wireless technology, all of these devices can be used to access and download information. Students also have access to an array of software that can perform complex calculations, simulations, and analyses at the push of a button. Finally, they have access to vast repositories of information via the Internet. While it is true that colleges cannot control students' access to computer and Internet technology, they can take concrete measures to ensure that the technology is used responsibly.

Educators need to be aware that all of these technologies can be used as either aids to learning or aids to cheating. As Renard (2000) pointed out, "Educators unaware of the possibilities and resources available to computer-age students are at the mercy of these technologically hip kids" (p. 2). Thus, today's instructors need to be well versed in

1. The kinds of electronic devices students are using and what their capabilities are.
2. What kinds of software are available, especially for the subject areas they teach in.
3. What general Internet resources are available (e.g., encyclopedias and search engines).
4. What specific Internet resources are available that pertain to their subject areas.

Goldsmith (1998) suggested the following ways for faculty and administrators to increase their awareness of what computer resources are available:

• Know what computer facilities are available on campus and what their network access capabilities are. (In this way, for example, instructors can guard against cheating in computer labs where students are working on assignments or taking tests.)

- Keep up-to-date on computer technology issues. Regularly consult library and computer center staff and the weekly technology section of the *Chronicle of Higher Education*. Join an on-campus or online faculty discussion group.
- Use security programs for computer test materials or files. Discuss security issues with students at the beginning of class. Regularly review the security procedures being used, and change passwords or have students change passwords frequently.
- Establish clear policies about the use of electronic devices during tests. Be explicit about what students are allowed to use during tests, and provide guidelines or restrictions for their use, if allowed. For example, if programmable calculators are permitted, do students have to demonstrate that the memories are cleared before an exam?
- Establish clear policies about the kinds of computer resources that are and are not authorized for use in specific contexts. These resources include databases, electronic networks such as tutorials and homework helpers, and software programs (online or on CD-ROM).

Some colleges have actually banned the use of some or all electronic devices in the classroom, at least during tests. But as Goldsmith (1998) suggested, because it is not realistic to assume that students do not or cannot get access to certain kinds of technologies, colleges should focus instead on ways in which their use can be monitored or controlled. O'Neil (2003) provided an example of an instructor who allowed but controlled the use of PDAs:

> For quizzes in his "Integrated Circuits" course at Dartmouth, Mr. Cooley has had his students work on PDAs that they had used throughout the semester. He posted the tests on a course Web site and designed an authentication code that allowed students to view and complete the exams only when they logged on from the proper classroom at a specific time. He says his system also keeps students from hunting for answers on the Web while they are taking the quiz. (p. 2)

One administrator recommended creating multiple versions of tests:

> By now, most professors have learned not to post answer keys—either online or outside of the classroom—until every student

has completed the exam. But in some large courses at the University of California at Berkeley, each student receives an exam with multiple-choice questions in randomly generated order. "No two students are getting the same test," says Alexander J. Cuthbert, director of educational technology at Berkeley's Digital Chemistry Project. Consequently, students who try to get around the university's no-electronics policy won't be able to pass answer keys back and forth on phones or PDAs. (O'Neil, 2003)

In "New Toys for Cheating Students," Batista (2000) speculated that it may not be too long before the very devices that now enable cheating will be used to prevent it:

With the advent of a data transmission standard called "short messaging service," students can silently beam test answers to each other on their personal digital assistants [PDAs]. More ambitious students can create their own database of notes, then access them during the test. The possibilities are endless. Most wireless industry experts, however, predict that someday teachers in secondary and higher education will administer tests on PDAs, formatting them so that every student has a different set of questions. Imagine how upset you'd be if the answer you received from your friend corresponded to a completely different question. (p. 1)

Use Technology to Detect Plagiarism

The most effective way of both detecting and discouraging what is perhaps the most prolific form of cheating—plagiarism—is to use the Internet. As O'Neil (2003) pointed out, "If students can use the Internet to cheat, professors can also use hi-tech methods to detect plagiarism by utilizing the many anti-plagiarism websites available" (p. 4). Fain and Bates (2005) recommended this general approach to locating work on the Internet that instructors suspect may be plagiarized:

- Search for the title of the student's paper (within quote marks). (Occasionally, students are not savvy enough to change the title.)

- Use a variety of search engines to search, within quotation marks, a unique string of words used in the student's paper.
- To search for papers plagiarized from published articles, use a full-text database such as InfoTrac, ProQuest, or Science Direct.
- Visit a site specifically developed to detect plagiarism. (See Table 4.2 for suggestions.)

I would add to this list another recommendation:

- For colleges that have writing labs, check students' papers against any papers used as examples in the lab's database.

Fain and Bates's (2005) *Cheating 101: Paper Mills and You*, from which most of the foregoing recommendations are derived, and which can be downloaded from the Web, also contains links to a variety of useful information, including lists of Internet term paper and plagiarism detection sites and tips on both detecting and combating plagiarized papers.

Plagiarism detection sites work in different ways, and many of them charge a fee. O'Neil explained how some of the sites function and noted a critical and ironic distinction between those sites that retain the papers that are submitted for authenticity and those that do not:

Turnitin.com … checks papers against public available websites and other electronic sources available to students. The service keeps student papers in order to enlarge its database of manuscripts, books, and journals. Other services, such as Copycatch and Eve2 run student papers through a computer program without holding on to the papers (Foster, 2002)…. Two online services that help professors check student papers for plagiarism, Plagiserve.com and Edutie.com, appear to have ties to websites that sell term papers to students. That has some professors worried that the two services might be secretly selling the very papers that they claim to check (Young, 2002). (O'Neil, 2003)

Faculty members have also developed practical solutions to thwart technology-aided cheating. One group of graduate professors devised their own unique method of combating test-taking plagiarism:

At the start of the final exam for "Principles of Accounting I," the team of professors who taught the popular course posted on its Web site an answer key loaded with false responses to the 30 multiple choice questions. As some 400 students deliberated over their answers, the exam proctors sat and watched—ignoring occasionally suspicious noises coming from a few cell phones.... When the professors then compared each student's paper with the false key, they found that a dozen tests [almost] matched the fake answers...there was only one reasonable explanation: 12 of the students had cheated.... All of the implicated students either admitted to using their Internet-enabled cell phones to look up the answer key online, or were convicted of having done so by a group of professors and students. Those students received a grade signifying "failure due to academic dishonesty." (Read, 2004, p. 1)

Table 4.2
Plagiarism Detection Web Sites

CopyCatch.com	www.copycatch.com
Edutie.com	www.edutie.com
EVE 2: Essay Verification System	www.canexus.com/eve
Glatt Plagiarism Systems	www.plagiarism.com
Integriguard.com	www.integriguard.com.
Plagiarism.org	http://plagiarism.org
Turnitin	www.turnitin.com
WCopyfind	http://plagiarism.phys.virginia.edu/Wsoftware.html
Word Check	www.wordchecksystems.com

Devise New Instructional Methods

As one may imagine, the actions of the graduate professors described in the last paragraph generated a certain amount of controversy. On their own campus, those professors were praised by some as heroes and accused by others of participating in entrapment. But the reverberations from their actions were felt nationwide as colleagues from both 2- and 4-year colleges and universities responded to what they had read in the *Chronicle of Higher Education*. One blamed "outmoded approaches to learning and assessment" and chided members of academe to "wake up and rethink how we design both learning activities and assessment methods" (Rimmington, 2004). He noted:

> In a world that demands good communication, teamwork, and Internet abilities and skills, what looks like cheating in the old paradigm is actually highly desirable behavior.... We need to change the way we do assessment so we can simultaneously measure both team and individual performance in an environment that allows ready access to information using wireless Internet devices. After all, we dealt with calculators by rethinking how we tested math students. We have designed tests that can be open book. We merely need an extension of such a redesign. (p. 1)

Another colleague also spoke to the need for rethinking instructional design and shared one of his techniques:

> Cheating has always happened, with or without technology. The pressure on students to get good grades and the expectations of some instructors for students to be walking libraries [only amplify] the problem.... I have found a very easy way to stop cheating on exams.... I allow students to prepare a single cheat sheet and bring it in to the exam. The cheat sheet must be handwritten and turned in with the exam. I also typically allow students to answer only some of the questions. This way they are not pressured to know everything, and weakness in one area will not have a negative influence on their grade. I find that good students produce some very interesting cheat sheets, while poor students seldom bring one to the exam. The students who do bring cheat sheets seldom use them. I have tricked my students into studying! (Burningham, 2004, pp. 1–2)

Yet another community college faculty member offered a commonsense approach:

> I am not terribly concerned about students' using technology during exams. In fact, most of my exams are open book, open notes, open computer.... I am sure there are exceptions, but in my field (computer skills and information technology), I have

found it relatively easy to write exams that test whether a student understands and can apply key concepts. If he or she cannot, then having a textbook or a Web site available is of limited value.

By key concepts, I mean those that I'd like students to remember in a couple of years. Not that they could necessarily put the concept to practical use before consulting a book or a Web site—but they'd remember that they need to consider (for example) balancing costs and risks when devising their network security policies. Then they could research the current best practices and put those to use.... I do warn my students in advance that I am very good at detecting answers that are too similar to have been written independently, and that I will not hesitate to give cheaters a zero on the exam. (Biddulph, 2004, p. 2)

In the literature, there is a good deal of evidence that most educators recommend modifying course and test designs as a meaningful and common-sense approach to discouraging and eliminating cheating. Faculty members need to reassess course requirements and learning objectives in light of easy access to technological resources and ensure that these resources are used in service of learning, not cheating. They need to develop alternatives to traditional fill-in-the-blank, multiple-choice, short response tests that make cheating so easy and do little to foster critical thinking skills.

Advocate for Academic Integrity Beyond the Campus

Support Stronger Legislation to Combat Plagiarism and Cheating

Colleges need to be aware that the so-called Internet cheat sites or term paper mills that enable students to plagiarize (knowingly or not) contribute significantly to the problem of academic dishonesty. As was discussed in chapter 1 (see page 15), cheat sites are proliferating: Late in 2001, the AP Business wire estimated 2.6 million hits a month on such sites (cited in Groark, Oblinger, & Choa, 2001), and one can only assume that traffic has increased since.

Cizek (2003) acknowledged that "perhaps due to the increasing frequency of cheating on tests and plagiarism, these topics have begun to receive more attention from legislative bodies and the courts" (p. 105). To prove his point, he outlined legislation passed by California, Texas, and Washington, all of which were "in response to the proliferation of term paper mills" (Cizek, 2003, pp. 105–106). Although that may seem heartening, the reality is that, as of October 2007, only 18 states had enacted legislation that makes the preparation of academic assignments for profit unlawful (see Table 4.3, page 104). (The Connecticut statute, which may be one of the most comprehensive, is excerpted in Table 4.4, page 107.) Cizek also noted that some states have also legislated against cheating by teachers themselves:

> Such cheating occurs … when a teacher inappropriately divulges the contents of a state-mandated examination to students, when the teacher uses inappropriate test preparation methods with students, or when a teacher alters a student's answers. One example of such legislation is found in the Ohio Revised Code, which states that "no person shall reveal to any student any specific question that the person knows is part of a [state-mandated] test … or in any other way assist a pupil to cheat on such a test" (§3319.151). (2003, pp. 107–108)

Are the extant laws sufficiently intimidating to shut down those who are making a career of proliferating academic dishonesty? Consider a story from *The Chronicle of Higher Education*:

> An administrator at South Plains College in Texas has issued a warning to businesses that sell term papers over the World Wide Web, notifying them that their practices may violate a new state law against profiting from plagiarism.

> Last week, James Taylor, vice president for academic affairs at the college, sent his warning by e-mail to dozens of Web sites with names like "Cheater.com," "Schoolsucks.com," and "Evil House of Cheat." The letter describes a new Texas law … that penalizes anyone who "prepares, sells, offers, or advertises for sale, or delivers to another person an academic product when the person knows, or should reasonably have known, that a person intends to submit or use the academic product to satisfy an academic requirement."

> Dr. Taylor's message states: "We strongly suggest that you refrain

from selling or exchanging term papers and other academic products to anyone in Texas, especially our service area." It went on to state that the college "will seek prosecution" of those who violate the law.

Some who received the letter called the new law a violation of their free-speech rights. Others say that many states have similar laws but that they comply by making their customers sign waivers promising not to use the work as their own.

Still others welcomed the publicity. "The louder the noise, the more hits I get," says Kenny Sahr, who runs Schoolsucks.com, which distributes term papers free online. Mr. Sahr says he makes money by selling advertising space on the site. Speaking of Dr. Taylor, Mr. Sahr says, "The more he talks, the more places in Europe I get to travel." (Young, 1997, p. 1)

In a 2007 *Villanova Law Review* article, "Facilitated Plagiarism: The Saga of Term-Paper Mills and the Failure of Legislation and Litigation to Control Them," Dickerson thoroughly reviewed the history of term-paper mills and legislative efforts to stop them. Dickerson also analyzed why legal enforcement has failed, citing factors including the following:

• Enforcement officials have more serious crimes to contend with; many consider plagiarism to be a victimless and relatively minor crime.
• Term-paper mills adapt easily to challenges, for example, by shutting down and reopening under another name and domain.
• It is often difficult to determine ownership of term-paper mills, and the sheer number of sites is daunting.
• Even without mills, students can find papers on the Internet, and it requires a lot of effort on the part of instructors to patrol students' work and determine what is and is not plagiarized.

"Some view the situation regarding term-paper mills, plagiarism and facilitated plagiarism as hopeless," Dickerson stated. But she continued, "Protecting academic integrity, however, is crucial to our educational system, and

Table 4.3

State Legislation Pertaining to Preparation and Sale of Papers

California

California Education Code

Title 3. Postsecondary Education

Division 5. General Provisions

Part 40. Donahoe Higher Education Act

Chapter 6. Academic Materials

§ 66400. Prohibition concerning preparation, sale and distribution of term papers or thesis

§ 66401. Statements regarding preparation

Colorado

Colorado Revised Statutes

Title 23. Higher Education and Vocational Training, State Universities and Colleges, General and Administrative

Article 4. Trafficking in Academic Materials

§ 23-4-103. Preparation, sale, and distribution of academic materials—advertising

Connecticut

Connecticut Annotated Statutes

Title 53. Crimes

Chapter 949b. Academic Crimes

§ 53-392a. Definitions.

§ 53-392b. Preparation of assignments for students attending educational institutions prohibited.

§ 53-392c. Excepted actions.

Florida

Florida Annotated Statutes

Title 46. Crimes (Chs. 775–896)

Chapter 877. Miscellaneous Crimes

§ 877.17. Works to be submitted by students without substantial alteration

Illinois

Illinois Compiled Statutes Annotated

Chapter 110. Higher Education, General Provisions, Academic Plagiarism Act

§ 110 ILCS 5/1. [public policy; injunctions]

Maine

Maine Revised Statutes

Title 17-A. Maine Criminal Code

Part 2. Substantive Offenses

Chapter 29. Forgery and Related Offenses

§ 705. Criminal simulation

Maryland

Annotated Code of Maryland (Education)

Division IV. Other Education Provisions

Title 26. Prohibitions and Penalties

Subtitle 2. Sales of Academic Papers

§ 26-201. Sales of academic papers

Massachusetts

Annotated Laws of Massachusetts

Part IV. Crimes, Punishments and Proceedings In Criminal Cases

Title I. Crimes and Punishments

Chapter 271. Crimes Against Public Policy

§ 50. Sales of themes, theses, etc., to be used by another for academic credit; taking educational examinations for another; penalties.

Nevada

Nevada Revised Statutes Annotated

Title 15. Crimes and Punishments.

Chapter 207. Miscellaneous Crimes.

§ 207.320. Preparation or sale of academic writings.

New Jersey

New Jersey Annotated Statutes

Title 18a. Education

Subtitle 1. Definitions; General Provisions

Chapter 2. General Provisions

§ 18a:2-3. Preparation, offering for sale of certain documents; penalty

New York

New York Consolidated Law Service

Education Law

Title 1. General Provisions

Article 5. University of the State of New York

Part 1. General Organization

§ 213-b. Unlawful sale of dissertations, theses and term papers

North Carolina

General Statutes of North Carolina

Chapter 14. Criminal Law

Subchapter 05. Offenses Against Property

Article 20. Frauds

§ 14-118.2. Assisting, etc., in obtaining academic credit by fraudulent means

Table 4.3 continued

Oklahoma
Oklahoma Statutes
Title 21. Crimes and Punishments
Part I. In General
Chapter 1. Preliminary Provisions
§ 2. Criminal acts are only those prescribed—"this code" defined

Texas
Texas Statutes and Codes (Penal Code)
Title 7. Offenses Against Property
Chapter 32. Fraud
Subchapter D. Other Deceptive Practices
§ 32.50. Deceptive preparation and marketing of academic product

Oregon
Oregon Revised Statutes
Title 16. Crimes and Punishments
Chapter 165. Offenses Involving Fraud or Deception
Business and Commercial Offenses
§165.114. Sale of educational assignments.

Virginia
Code of Virginia
Title 18.2. Crimes and Offenses Generally
Chapter 12. Miscellaneous
Article 3. Miscellaneous Offenses In General
§ 18.2-505. Preparation, etc., of papers to be submitted for academic credit

Pennsylvania
Pennsylvania Consolidated Statutes
Title 18. Crimes and Offenses
Part II. Definition of Specific Offenses
Article G. Miscellaneous Offenses
Chapter 73. Trade and Commerce
Subchapter A. Definition of Offenses Generally
§ 7324. Unlawful sale of dissertations, theses and term papers

Washington
Annotated Revised Code of Washington
Title 28b. Higher Education
Chapter 28b.10. Colleges and Universities Generally
§ 28b.10.580. Term papers, theses, dissertations, sale of prohibited—legislative findings—purpose
§ 28b.10.582. Term papers, theses, dissertations, sale of prohibited—definitions
§ 28b.10.584. Term papers, theses, dissertations, sale of prohibited—violations enumerated—exempted acts—civil penalties—injunctive relief

to society in general." She concluded with this recommendation:

Going forward, legislative and judicial action should not be abandoned. Colleges must recognize, however, that legal action, in isolation, will not stop term-paper mills and will not curb the larger issue of academic dishonesty. Instead, colleges should consider adopting, for academic dishonesty issues, the environmental management model that has proven successful in addressing public-health challenges, such as alcohol and other drug prevention on college campuses. Under this model, schools should take a comprehensive, coordinated, science-based approach to tackling matters of academic dishonesty. Steps under this paradigm include problem identification, outcome identification, research, collaborative problem-solving, program implementation and evaluation. (Dickerson, 2007)

Clearly, much more needs to be done to curtail illegal sales of academic work. Colleges need to adopt comprehensive strategies that create a climate of integrity in which academic dishonesty is made difficult to thrive. Leaders from local, state, and national accrediting agencies; state coordinating and governing bodies; faculty governing bodies and bargaining units; student groups; and community college trustees also need to work together to demand strengthened laws to allow for the prosecution of those who facilitate, and profit from the perpetuation of, plagiarism and cheating.

Get Involved on a National Level

There exists no community college–based organization designed to assist community colleges in focusing national attention on the issue of academic integrity. However, community colleges may consider membership in CAI, which may prove helpful for those colleges looking for background information and opportunities for professional development relevant to academic integrity. The CAI Web site provides numerous valuable resources, including sample documents, resource lists, and links to featured institutions. (Readers will note that membership in CAI is one of the primary recommendations emerging from the case studies presented in chapter 5.) For those seeking a general how-to approach to promoting academic integrity, CAI's Academic Integrity Assessment Guide may be particularly useful (see www.academicintegrity.org/assessment_guide/index.php). The guide contains the following resources:

- Survey instruments for students and faculty. (McCabe compiles survey data and provides a customized, confidential report.)
- Guidelines for appointing an academic integrity assessment committee.
- Step-by-step instructions for a comprehensive assessment process that includes policies and practices, educational programs, and sanctions.
- Suggested assessment and educational activities and questions for focus groups.
- Examples of codes and policies from campuses across the country.
- Copies of relevant reading materials and bibliographies.

Table 4.4

Excerpts From the Connecticut Statutes Pertaining to Academic Crimes

---

Title 53, Chapter 949b: Academic Crimes
§ 53-392a. Definitions.

As used in this chapter: "Person" means any individual, partnership, corporation, limited liability company or association; "assignment" means any specific written, recorded, pictorial, artistic or other academic task that is intended for submission to any university, college, academy, school or other educational institution which is chartered, incorporated, licensed, registered or supervised by this state, in fulfillment of the requirements of a degree, diploma, certificate or course of study at any such educational institution; and "prepare" means to create, write or in any way produce in whole or substantial part a term paper, thesis, dissertation, essay, report or other written, recorded, pictorial, artistic or other assignment for a fee.

---

§ 53-392b. Preparation of assignments for students attending educational institutions prohibited.

(a) No person shall prepare, offer to prepare, cause to be prepared, sell or offer for sale any term paper, thesis, dissertation, essay, report or other written, recorded, pictorial, artistic or other assignment knowing, or under the circumstances having reason to know, that said assignment is intended for submission either in whole or substantial part under the name of a student other than the author of the term paper, thesis, dissertation, essay, report or other written, recorded, pictorial, artistic or other assignment in fulfillment of the requirements for a degree, diploma, certificate or course of study at any university, college, academy, school or other educational institution which is chartered, incorporated, licensed, registered or supervised by this state.

(b) Nothing contained in this chapter shall prevent any person from providing tutorial assistance, research material, information or other assistance to persons enrolled in a university, college, academy, school or other educational institution which is chartered, incorporated, licensed, registered or supervised by this state, which is not intended for submission directly or in substantial part as an assignment under the student's name to such educational institution in fulfillment of the requirements for a degree, diploma, certificate or course of study or to prevent any person from rendering for a fee services which include the typing, research, assembling, transcription, reproduction or editing of a manuscript or other assignment which he has not prepared at the request of or on behalf of the purchaser.

---

§ 53-392c. Excepted actions.

Nothing contained in this chapter shall prevent any person from selling or offering for sale a publication or other written material which shall have been registered under the United States laws of copyright, provided the owner of such copyright shall have given his authorization or approval for such sale and provided such publication or other written material shall not be intended for submission as a dissertation, thesis, term paper, essay, report or other written assignment to an educational institution within the state of Connecticut in fulfillment of the requirements for a degree, diploma, certificate or course of study.

---

§ 53-392e. Unlawful preparation of academic assignments: Class B misdemeanor.

Any person who violates any provision of this chapter shall be guilty of a class B misdemeanor. Any court of competent jurisdiction may grant such further relief as is necessary to enforce the provisions of this chapter, including the issuance of an injunction

---

Conduct More Research Specific to Community Colleges

More needs to be learned about the nature and frequency of academic dishonesty specifically within the nation's community colleges and about the perceptions and actions of community college students, faculty, administrators, and trustees. As has been stated repeatedly throughout this book, most of the research on academic dishonesty has been focused on 4-year institutions (or high schools). Community colleges differ from 4-year institutions in some significant ways; therefore, we should not assume that all extant research on the subject is generalizable to them. National research should be undertaken to determine the frequency of the problem within community colleges, to identify the issues that contribute to its occurrence, and—most important—to determine the organizational responses that may be effective in creating and promoting a culture of integrity (i.e., identify best practices).

One of the most significant differences between community colleges and 4-year institutions is the students. Any given classroom of community college students is likely to be far more diverse in terms of age, race and ethnicity, employment status, attendance status, and education goals than is a classroom of typical freshmen at a 4-year institution. Given that fundamental difference, obvious questions about community college students arise. Are they more honest or less honest than their 4-year counterparts? Do they rationalize and diminish academic dishonesty with the same apparent abandon of students in high schools and universities? Are their motivations the same as those of other students? More important, how do generational differences come into play within the more diverse community college classroom?

At the institutional level, other obvious questions arise. Is academic dishonesty as serious an issue in community colleges as it is in other education institutions? Are community college faculty and administrators handling the issue any better or worse? Findings from Aaron and Georgia (1994) and Aaron (1992) have suggested that community colleges have been less effective at detecting and dealing with academic dishonesty than have 4-year institutions. Burke's (1997) research yielded some contradictory findings: On the one hand, faculty surveyed did not perceive academic dishonesty to be a serious problem. On the other hand, the majority of them (65%–80%) acknowledged its occurrence, did not have or follow an institutional policy, and believed that students were primarily responsible for reducing academic dishonesty.

More and newer data are clearly needed, but perhaps with a slightly different focus. As Higbee and Thomas (2002) asserted, "Researchers can no longer limit their focus to who cheats or why students cheat, or whether academic honesty is on the rise or the decline. It is imperative that educators conduct further studies to explore how students and faculty define academic honesty and share their findings with both groups" (cited in Wotring, 2007).

Conclusion

A college's failure to promote academic integrity as a priority actually perpetuates the problem. Without an organized effort, community colleges are less likely to develop policies to support academic integrity or address academic dishonesty. The absence of such policies makes it impossible for colleges to respond appropriately, which can mean the difference between liability and effective resolution. Given the scarcity of funds on many community college campuses, money is available only for activities deemed "mission critical." One can only imagine the inertia within community colleges if the central mission of teaching and learning received the relatively scant attention that academic dishonesty receives. Although community college personnel do not need more stress, the only thing worse than an apparent ethics crisis among their students is the future of their institutions if they do nothing. In the next chapter, I present case studies of four colleges that have made academic integrity a priority on their campuses.

CHAPTER FIVE

Promoting Academic Integrity: Four Success Stories

Introduction

In the March 31, 2003, edition of *The New Yorker*, cartoonist Bruce Eric Kaplan offered a satirical commentary on the capricious nature of motivation. In his cartoon, two horses stand facing each other in a hillside corral, with one horse saying to the other: "Really, only you can tell yourself to giddyup." Anyone who has struggled to work up the will to face a challenging task inevitably faces the moment when it is easier to give in than it is to go on. Gratefully, this was not the case with the four community colleges I profile in this chapter, as both the profiles and the recommendations at the end of the chapter will show. The four colleges are as follows:

- North Harris Community College, Houston, Texas
- Oakton Community College, Des Plaines, Illinois
- Pueblo Community College, Pueblo, Colorado
- Temple College, Temple, Texas

Even though only four colleges are highlighted, they are representative of different regions of the United States as well as different sizes of institutions. And regardless of differences in size and geography and the specific problems each college faced, they all have several things in common. The first is the desire to raise awareness of the importance of academic integrity within their colleges. The second is a demonstrated commitment to addressing academic dishonesty through concrete actions. Finally, each college has acknowledged that the one way to stem the rising tide of academic dishonesty is to emphasize integrity. Presenting only four profiles is not to suggest that many other community colleges are not engaged in promoting academic integrity. The colleges highlighted here are intended to serve as but four examples of good and thoughtful practice and to provide an opportunity for readers to learn from the experience of colleagues.

The profiles presented in this chapter are based on personal interviews the author conducted with community college administrators and faculty members in fall 2005. The comments quoted are taken from unpublished transcripts of these interviews, edited only to effect continuity and clarity.

North Harris Community College

With a background in business and industry, Melanie Jacks Hilburn (currently the director of professional development and training and a full-time faculty member) embraced the opportunity to teach developmental reading at the oldest of five colleges in the North Harris Montgomery Community College system in Houston, Texas. Asked to describe how the college and the district became involved in the discussion of ethics, Hilburn recalled a visit by Rush Kidder, founder of the Institute for Global Ethics (IGE), who was invited by the district's chancellor to speak at convocation. "I was looking for a professional development opportunity," Hilburn (personal communication, September 17, 2005) began. "I went to the IGE Web site and was able to sell the president on sending me to training." She continued,

> When you go away for professional development, and you get money to go, you have to share what you learned. So on conference day, I did a session. The purpose was to bring up the topic and start a discussion. I recruited some people to help me, and we did a focus group to find out what people thought of the ethical climate at the college. We looked at what people were interested in doing, and that is when I established the roundtable discussions and started doing ethics training. Then we looked at the district's ethics policy and asked how many people knew we had one.

> Well, only the vice president, the dean, and the faculty senate president were familiar with it. A lot of people thought, "Well, that's the district's policy." So we began to talk about what our own policy would look like—a separate ethical code for the college—and we came up with our core values. Then we did the same thing for our instructional leadership group and a couple of other groups. And you know, the more we do, the more we see ethics raised to a level of awareness we never had before. The other day, I told someone casually that I was going to leave a little early—15 minutes—to go to a hair appointment, and someone perked up and asked, "Is that ethical?"

Hilburn is justifiably proud of having incorporated ethics into developmental reading courses for her students, many of whom are unfamiliar with the concept of ethics or the role it plays in their lives, in or out of the learning environment. "They didn't realize that if the person at the bank gave you $300 too much money, it was wrong to keep it," she said, continuing,

> I began to integrate what I had learned at the ethics institute into my developmental courses. A teacher can use almost anything as long as the students are reading. So I took the seminar and integrated it into my critical reading series. It was astonishing that they had never been introduced to these principles before. So I began to use this ethical fitness curriculum that first teaches them how to look at what their values systems are, how to identify ethical dilemmas, how to find a process for resolving them. So they had to apply this to real-life situations.

> Another student who had gone through this training once told me that he had no idea how unethical he was. He told me a story of how he had witnessed his best friend commit a rape in high school and how he had said nothing to the police. He didn't deny it, he told me. He just basically said, "I don't know" and walked away. He told me that it never dawned on him that what he was doing was wrong and that he didn't know how he had wound up so lost. He told me that he had good parents—his father was an executive with a homebuilding company—and a good family. He had no idea how he got to where he was. So it was so fulfilling to have students like him go through this and then tell me how they had used it since then. I saw them take it out and apply it. It was very successful.

In her first week of class, Hilburn organizes an event she calls "Building Academic Community." To develop a code of personal ethical behavior applicable to academics, she asks her students to reflect on their past behaviors and the past behaviors of others, specifically their instructors:

> I put them into groups and ask them to talk among themselves about things that have prevented them from being successful. And, of course, they come up with people who aren't respectful or who come in late. Then I ask them, "What does a positive student

look like or act like?" Then I have them do the same thing from a teacher's perspective and ask, "What have instructors done to help you?" Well, in effect, what happens at the end is that they have built a code of ethics for their class that they agree to abide by throughout the semester and that they hold each other to.

It is critical to let students know your expectations. The ethical issues that come up in our classrooms have occurred because we have not communicated our expectations to students. As a faculty member of this college—and as an employee of the district— I have a responsibility for the moral education and moral remediation of our students.

Summary of Actions Taken

Over time, what began as simple roundtable discussions at the college developed into several large-scale, campuswide events, including the following:

- Using materials borrowed from Hilburn to raise her students' awareness of integrity, English teacher Joyce Boatright developed her freshman composition curriculum around an ethics theme.
- The college developed "Ethical Awareness Week" to involve faculty, staff, administrators, and students in activities including a film club showing of a movie with an ethical theme (and follow-up discussion group), library-sponsored workshops on plagiarism (for students and faculty), job center workshops on ethical interviewing, mini-seminars in a variety of classes and program areas across campus, student newspaper interviews and articles, and a poster campaign and a t-shirt fundraiser benefiting the college scholarship fund.

Hilburn credited her colleagues and the support of the college community in the development of those activities, saying that nothing like this can take place without the common effort of many faculty members, administration employees, and students. She mentioned with special fondness the assistance of her president:

Our president, Dr. David Sam, is the best. He has supported me 100%. I can remember when I wanted to go to that training—my dean gave me $1,500, and the faculty senate gave me the same or a bit more, but it was very expensive. So when I was applying, I remember people saying, "You are never going to get that money." But I was a salesman in my past life and I thought, "Hey, you don't ask for it, you don't get it." So I got it and I went up there and got the training and when I came back, Dr. Sam gave me free reign.

When I wanted to go back up the next year to attend a symposium on communicating ethics, he wrote the $3,500 check out of his own budget. Anything I want to do to promote this, he is supportive of. He is a man of integrity, and I think that is why he is so supportive. There might be other places where presidents are not so ethical, and they might not be so willing to embrace it. I spoke at the NISOD convention this year, and he made a point to come and to attend the session. He was there to support me and to come up afterwards and give me a big bear hug and say, "Thank you so much. You made me proud." I felt so good about that. It's more about the little things and not the money. It's knowing how much he cares that makes me want to care even more.

Even someone of Hilburn's amazing energy and entrepreneurial style is not indefatigable. "This summer, I was just burned out. My position used to have only four programs, and now there are seventeen." She elaborated:

I thought, "Okay. I can't do everything. I'll maintain the Web site, but not worry about the ethics thing. I am going to move that to the bottom of my list." And then I got back to school, and I had a call from people in the custodial department. They would like a workshop for their staff because they are having some issues. The Chamber of Commerce called and asked if I would do a presentation for them. It just revives me because I see the need for an ethics program. More than anything, people do see the value in it, and they do want it, and I do need to continue to carry it forward. I began to realize that this is what my calling is on this campus. It became my passion. This is how I am able to use my gift of influence and change things on the campus.

Oakton Community College

In the fall semester of 2000, professor Bill Taylor, who retired in 2006, found himself being interviewed by the *Chicago Tribune*. He had not received an award or authored an enormous research grant. He was not leading a charge against anything or signed up to address the board of trustees. What had he done? He had written a letter to his students. Granted, it was a lengthy letter and filled with scholarly advice, but is that newsworthy? It is if you work for "one of the few community colleges in the nation active in the work of the [Center for Academic Integrity], a consortium of about 200 colleges and universities that promotes the values of honesty, trust, fairness, respect, and responsibility in academia" (Allen, 2000, p. 1).

The reporter described the actions of Taylor (who taught government at Oakton for more than 30 years), the activities of his colleagues at Oakton Community College, and the actions of their students:

> Faculty members at Oakton are given brochures on how to deter cheating, recommending specific techniques for handling exams and term papers. A handout for students titled "Cheating: A Way to Ruin Your College Career" lists types of cheating and penalties. Even class syllabuses include anti-cheating codes.

> But Taylor has gone a step further. At the start of his courses, he distributes a six-page personal letter to students explaining the concept of academic integrity and spelling out point by point the standards of conduct he expects. Then he devotes an entire class period to discussing the issue.

> His approach has won him some small renown. He said about 100 colleagues in community colleges around the country requested full copies of his letter after a portion appeared recently in a national teaching publication.

> The letter asks, "Would you want to be operated on by a doctor who cheated his way through medical school? Or would you be comfortable on a bridge designed by an engineer who cheated her way through engineering school? Would you trust your tax return to an accountant who copied his exam answers from his neighbor?"

But after discussing the issue with his students this fall, he's discouraged. "They seem to feel that cheating in small things is unrelated to cheating in other things." Taylor said. "And they have a notion that in public life, if you don't lie or cheat or deceive, you wouldn't get anywhere because they all do it." (Allen, 2000, p. 2)

Asked to describe the evolution of the letter, Taylor credited the seminal contributions of Mary Adams, whom he described as having opened the door to the college's participation in CAI:

She asked me if I would be interested in coming to one of their annual conferences, and I did and I loved it. The focus was very important for me, and the students were there. In fact, there were more students there than nonstudents or faculty and administrators, and there they were—a very inspirational bunch in terms of what they do at their schools to promote academic integrity.

I'm not sure if it was the first year of the CAI, but Don McCabe and a few other people had been working on a statement of principles with respect to academic integrity. It struck me that the things we were expecting of students were things that a faculty member with integrity is also doing. Also, it occurred to me that one of the problems with talking about academic integrity is that it tends to come across as something we're doing to them, as if we were saying, "We're going to prevent you from cheating." Of course, that's true, but over the years, there have been a number of discussions about the "two-pronged" approach to academic integrity.

On the one hand, there's how you prevent cheating, and on the other hand, there's how you promote integrity and not just prevent cheating in any one classroom. The first is important, but I am more interested in the second. It occurred to me that if I could let students know and understand the nature of academic integrity as it is a part of the academic enterprise—and for both of us—then we'd stand a better chance of convincing them that it was something to believe in. So, I got to thinking about how all of these things applied to me as well as to them, and the letter evolved. It is an attempt to show students that they and I both live by this principle. (W. Taylor, personal communication, September 12, 2005)

Taylor acknowledged a productive working relationship that is characteristic of the college, adding that the rapport between faculty and both the vice presidential and presidential levels only enhanced the college's ability to effectively address and promote academic integrity:

I came to Oakton at the end of its first year as a college. It has always been a school where there has been a good relationship, a cooperative relationship between the faculty and administration. And that's a tremendous credit to both groups. There's never been any doubt that our former vice president, Mary Olson, was committed to integrity. She'd been a founding board member of CAI and developed a policy very early on as a result of her involvement. She knew that the old way of doing things—with the teacher tearing up the fraudulent paper—wouldn't work.

Taylor also credited the character of the college's president, Margaret "Peg" Lee, for the college's strong and active stance in the promotion of integrity, both in and out of the classroom:

We all know about or hear about administrators who override the faculty, or who ignore faculty complaints about integrity and all that. And if you have a president who has that attitude, then the vice president is one whose area is critical to academic integrity, and faculty members are going to be on a limb if he or she does not reflect the president's feelings. So it goes unaddressed. But fortunately, that wasn't our fate. You'd have to know Peg. She was the vice president for academic affairs and was there since the mid-1980s, and she is a very loving, caring, and ethical person. She was very much committed to values. It was a positive environment for talking about this kind of issue.

The positive environment described by Taylor produced several significant activities designed to address and promote academic integrity, some of which were the individual efforts of Oakton faculty members, and some of which involved the faculty as a whole. His original letter (see Appendix A), which was intended to model the integrity he expected to see in his students, also inspired the creation of a statement adopted by all Oakton faculty members in which they elaborated on the expectations and activities of faculty members and their obligation to contribute to the culture of academic integrity. The statement, "Promoting Integrity in Academic Life and Beyond" is posted on Oakton's server under "New Faculty Resources" as "Academic Integrity 'Best Practices' Document" (see Appendix B).

A statement this powerful has an undeniable effect because it speaks to and demonstrates a clear intention to promote and uphold the principles of integrity in the learning environment. Lee acknowledged the significance of the efforts of a few faculty leaders and described the organizational effect those efforts have on the climate of the college:

> The person responsible for advancing the agenda of academic integrity at Oakton was then-VP for Student Affairs, Dr. Mary Olson. Mary was one of the founding members and first community college person on the board of CAI. She herself was a model of the integrity she advocated and was held in high esteem by all of her peers. Mary involved Bill Taylor, who is now retired, as well as Lynda Jerit (also retired). Bill and Lynda were highly respected teachers and leaders among the faculty and were two of the five faculty architects of Oakton's FIPSE-funded critical literacy program. With this and the academic integrity initiative, they transformed teaching and learning at Oakton and have also touched many minds and hearts beyond Oakton and even beyond Illinois.

> Our newer faculty member, Dr. Mary Johanssen Schmidt, has also been involved with the CAI. She is co-chairing the college's self-study now in process and was recognized several weeks ago as the outstanding faculty member for the year—a very prestigious award and very well deserved—she is an outstanding teacher— like Bill Taylor. The legacy of Mary Olson, Bill, and Lynda has continued in Mary Johanssen Schmidt and with so many of our faculty, staff, and administrators. It echoes in Oakton's statement

of mission, vision, and core values—which are available on our Web site (www.oakton.edu/visitor/mission.htm). If words can capture the heart of a culture, I believe these words do. (M. Lee, personal communication, September 12, 2005)

Summary of Actions Taken

Oakton Community College engages in the following activities to promote academic integrity:

- Students receive a handout educating them on the ways that academic dishonesty can negatively affect their college career.
- Faculty members receive brochures outlining methods for deterring academic dishonesty and enforcing integrity on exams and written assignments.
- Course syllabi include the college's academic dishonesty policy.
- Many Oakton faculty members send their students a personal letter regarding academic integrity, explaining how they (faculty), too, are expected to function in a culture of honesty and asking their students to do likewise.
- Faculty members have developed a statement that outlines and pledges to support and model principles of integrity and the behavior expected of students in the learning environment.
- Oakton's board of trustees approves a statement of mission, vision, and values that purposefully incorporates language referencing their desire to develop students as learners who "apply ethical principles in their academic, work and personal lives" and that demands from the students—as well as from themselves—tolerance, fairness, responsibility, and integrity (see Oakton Community College, 2001).

Asked to describe the necessary elements that preclude such an intense variety of activity, Lee speculated that commitment to something larger than any one individual or any one campus was the lynchpin of the campuses' action. "I think the necessary elements are unshakable commitment and a common vision," she began. "Something bigger than everybody. Something that is purposefully transformative in the students' lives and in the lives of those who are serving students—faculty, staff, and administrators." She paused and then added, "It takes a commitment to do the right thing because it is the right thing" (M. Lee, personal communication, September 12, 2005).

Pueblo Community College

In 1995, Dennis Johnson, a student development administrator at Pueblo Community College, went to an annual training session at the Association for Student Judicial Affairs. There, he met Sally Cole, who led a presentation on academic integrity. "I was just overwhelmed," he began, "by this radical group that was trying to change campus cultures. I brought that back to the college and said, 'This is something we really need to be a part of.'" He continued, "I discussed it with our dean and the vice president, and they agreed" (D. Johnson, personal communication, September 4, 2005).

With administrative buy-in established, Johnson went about the business of creating consensus among the faculty and students, garnering support from the instructors and honor student organization, Phi Theta Kappa. In the years that followed, their activities expanded from one department to across the campus. Johnson described the evolution of the focus on academic integrity:

> One of the big things we realized was we needed to get faculty on board, so we worked with the English Department. During all of the composition courses for one semester, they took on the theme of academic integrity. If they were doing their argumentative paper or the various types of papers in the composition classes, if it was possible, they used the theme of integrity or one of the principles of the fundamental values of integrity and had students write about that.

But their activities did not focus solely on students; the emphasis on integrity began to reflect the purposeful involvement of the faculty:

> We sent various materials to the faculty members like the "Ten Principles of Integrity" that Gary Pavela and Don McCabe had put together. Then, for the whole campus, we organized an Integrity Week and had various activities. We are not a residential campus, so it is a little harder to get students to stay for activities, but we have a fall festival and a spring fling as a fun day, and we decided to promote academic integrity at those events. We've had a pledge drive where we have asked people to uphold the principles of integrity; we gave them cards and different things. We have three different poster campaigns on campus emphasizing integrity

and whenever I find something on integrity, I send it to our faculty and I get a fair amount—not a whole lot—but a fair amount of appreciation in feedback for that.

Listing other specific activities sponsored by Pueblo Community College, Johnson added:

We've been able to get a statement into all syllabi about academic integrity, and we are promoting that as a campus. We ask all of our faculty to highlight that on the first day (of classes) when they are going over the syllabus with the students. That's what we stand for. Looking at the positive. But it also lets them know that we will do the "policing."

Johnson also does presentations in campus-based professional development seminars for the faculty and for student services personnel. His college has not overlooked one of the most typically forgotten constituencies: associate faculty members. He explained:

We have ongoing faculty development, so throughout the semester, we have a variety of presentations where different faculty members and student services members are present. We are also doing this with our part-time faculty. Two thirds of our faculty are part time, so we have started doing more faculty development. A major part was a presentation on student discipline, and it emphasized academic integrity with the part-time instructors.

This foray into the promotion of academic integrity—from the perspective of a student development staff member—has been unpredictable, at best:

I was really interested in disruptive classroom behavior. When I came back from a conference in 1996, I started putting together some guides for faculty to understand the student discipline process. They loved it. A month later, I put together one on academic dishonesty and got crucified because faculty felt that it was their domain. Disruption—that's student behavior; that's my area. But integrity and cheating—that's the faculty's domain. And it wasn't everybody, but a number of very vocal faculty members said, "You don't have anything to do with that. Student judicial affairs has nothing to do with cheating in the classroom."

Even more surprising, Johnson encountered faculty members who not only wanted to ensure their territorial rights but also saw no particular need to address the issue of academic integrity. He noted,

> One of our faculty and I had this wonderful discussion. He did not care if students cheated. He was a math teacher and he said, "You know, eventually, it'll catch up with them." I said that we want to be promoting integrity and values and not just letting people think cheating was okay. But his opinion was that we just shouldn't be talking about this. So, I took it a little slower and started going to a few key faculty members and gradually started building this process rather than just think that everybody is going to accept this immediately. So, for the last seven or eight years, it has been building slowly, but the dialogue has involved the entire campus. I think it's a much healthier way than to say that the judicial affairs office is opposing cheating or even some administrator saying that you must do this. It's come from the faculty and the students that this is what we want to be—an institution of integrity.

Johnson admitted that the college adjudicates about five or six integrity incidents per semester but added that it was not overly common. Addressing the typical tension between academicians and student services personnel, his comments reflect balance of philosophy and the kind of pragmatic observation that results from experience:

> I have seen it exist. That was the tension I talked about. "This is ours. You stay out of it. If we have a behavior problem, you can help us with that, but you stay out of all this academic stuff." Cheating is a behavior problem, and we need to work together on that. I think, over time, one thing that helped us resolve the distance between the two worlds is that I began teaching. And so now, I am seen as a faculty member as well. And I think that makes a difference. But over time, whenever a faculty member

would come forward with a case and see how fair we were, both to the faculty member and the student, and how we looked for substantial evidence and refused to take one side or the other, many faculty saw and appreciated and respected that.

Also responsible for the activities of the student judicial affairs group that adjudicated disciplinary problems with students, Johnson preferred to emphasize the promotion of integrity over the policing of academic dishonesty:

We are utilizing the developmental model and the educational process and not just kicking students out. Too many have grown up in that culture that just allows this or says we don't want to talk about it. And they are seeing that we are talking about it and trying to change the way we deal with it. I think the educational part can build, but it does take time and student services and faculty must achieve a partnership.

What Pueblo Community College has done results from effective partnering between student development personnel, faculty members, and students. If they can do it, what explains the general absence of community colleges from membership in groups such as CAI? Johnson suggested,

Because we work in community colleges, we have so many different jobs. For example, student discipline is one part of my job, but I am doing advising and registration. I am doing high school programs and all of these other things. Both student services and administration have so much to do that it is hard to find time to look at one more thing. Integrity is important, but I have seven other committees that I am serving on. I don't have time to address this. Other student judicial affairs officers might say, "Great idea." But 10 minutes later, they are dealing with the other administrative parts of their job, and integrity fades into another day. Many universities have a larger staff and people designated to concentrate on these issues and recognize the need, so integrity becomes a part of their job. We have to make the time, and we don't have an abundance of that.

As much as he decries the overall lack of time so common to community college professionals, Johnson has not stopped taking an additional step to promote academic integrity. He described the latest partnership with the local high school in developing a character education campaign that incorporates business and industry leaders from the community to support integrity:

> One of the local schools was talking about initiating a character education program seven years ago. This school was putting together a business education partnership, and both the high school and the business community were recognizing the issue of character as important. They began doing things together to promote character. This year, we are going to have our second annual character celebration, bringing high school students to the college campus and bringing in speakers and other groups to reinforce the value of integrity.

Summary of Actions Taken

Pueblo Community College engages in the following activities to promote integrity:

- Membership in CAI
- Completion of a campuswide integrity audit (using CAI surveys to gather student and faculty data regarding academic dishonesty)
- Involvement within the English Department that resulted in writing assignments focused on integrity
- Development of brochures for full- and part-time faculty members promoting academic integrity and detection of academic dishonesty
- Campuswide poster campaigns emphasizing the importance of academic integrity
- Inclusion of an academic integrity policy into course syllabi
- Faculty-led discussions with students on the topic of integrity on the first day of classes
- Professional development activities for full- and part-time faculty, as well as student services staff, focusing on academic integrity
- Promotional activities focusing on integrity incorporated into college events (fall festival and spring fling)
- Partnership activities with local business, industry, and educational institutions that focus on character education

Temple College

The issue of academic dishonesty is not unfamiliar to Sarah Nell Summers, a member of the faculty at Temple College and chairman of the Performing Arts Department. Summers, who was appointed to the college's Academic Integrity Task Force in 2004 and asked to chair it by the college's vice president of educational services, could not have found a deeper niche if she had carved it out herself. "If I had my way," she observed, "we'd have a flag out there on the flag pole next to the Texas flag and the U.S. flag. It'd have two words on it: *Prize Integrity*. And we'd be flying it day and night" (S. N. Summers, personal communication, September 17, 2005).

Asked to describe activities at the college that have promoted integrity, Summers replied:

> We began several years ago with a concern that our students needed an infusion of ethics in every part of the curriculum. I gathered a group of people together with our VP of student services, and we began thinking of ways that we could put a unit of ethics in every single course on campus. We got a lot of resistance because the teachers felt that there was too much to cover in their courses already. Others said that they already taught ethics as it applied in their subject area. But our committee felt that this was really not enough. We felt that teaching ethics as a part of a specific curriculum came too late in the student's academic career. Anyway, it never really went anywhere because we kept running into a lot of negative thinking—people just didn't want to buy what we had to sell—so some of us started to re-think it.

Not one to confuse retreat with loss, Summers began to document things she would occasionally hear spoken of quietly among colleagues:

> I was hearing about really stupid things students did to copy another person's work or foolish things that they thought they could get away with. And after a while, I started to hear things that I thought were more serious. Faculty members were finding papers that students had found on the Internet, or they were encountering sources that were unexplainable. I even received a

paper with three separate pages on three separate cites that had nothing to do with each other just stapled together with a cover sheet. I had to confront the student—who was twice my size—who couldn't defend or explain what he'd turned in.

Wisely, Summers routinely asked her students not only to write a term paper, but also to be prepared to present it in class. This particular student was so lost on the topic that his illicit academic activity was apparent to even his classmates. Eventually, he failed the course and contested his grade, but the worst was yet to come. Summers was called to task for not specifying that the work her students were expected to do reflect their own original effort.

"I had trouble getting backing on my decision to fail him, because my syllabus did not say that it had to be his own work," she said. Some people asked if she had expressly stated that the work must be his own or had implied it. Sadly, she had presumed the integrity of production and had not, in fact, specifically cautioned against any of the illicit methods she knew existed. Even more disappointing was the reaction of some of her colleagues and former members of instructional leadership. She had been prepared for the student to contest the grade, but she was quite unprepared to defend herself against those leaders who would intimate that she—as the teacher—was somehow to blame for an act of dishonesty because she had not specifically prohibited it. She recalled,

> He got an *F*, and he was livid. He had turned in a paper; that was supposed to be enough. It didn't have to be his work. I hadn't specified that it had to be authentic work. To me, I thought that was a given in academics, but to his mind, it wasn't. He had paid for the class, and as such, he could produce the paper however he chose as long as he turned in a paper.

Even when faculty members began to revise their first-day handouts to include an ethics statement and an explanation of how they would handle incidents of academic dishonesty, Summers was not entirely comfortable with the situation. "I felt as if I was hanging out there on my own little branch," she explained. "And all of the other faculty were on their own little branches too. But none of us were connected to anything." Logically, she began to research the college's scholastic integrity policy, which she believed needed improvement. She explained,

I read our integrity policy, and it was really inadequate. It didn't address all of the issues. It didn't speak of punishment in any effective way. It actually started off in a sentence that made it sound as if the only thing the college was interested in was not copying off another student's work. It was a "thou shalt not" but nothing would have happened if you did. There were anecdotes floating around campus about teachers who had discovered students who had cheated and teachers who had not been supported in their efforts to respond. But rather than lose faith in the system, some of us just decided to change the system.

Slightly more than one year later, Summers found herself interviewing with a new vice president for the position of chair of her department. In the conversation, the topic turned to her desire to address the problem of academic dishonesty. She remembered,

I mentioned that my main concern was that we establish an Academic Integrity Committee as a way to begin to protect the honest students. We needed to fix what seemed to be an increasingly difficult problem before the college encountered the kind of scandal I had heard about at other institutions. Three people from the original group joined the committee, and three more were appointed from the remaining divisions. I also asked one of the coaches to serve because they were as concerned about the honesty of their student athletes as we were.

At the end of the first meeting, each of us went back to our divisions and asked our colleagues—not just the full-time faculty, but the part-time faculty too—what they thought about the issue of dishonesty. We wanted to know if they felt an increase in the amount of cheating they saw. By the time we got back together for our next meeting, we had consensus. The campus was ready to do something.

Before the actual work of their committee began, Summers and the other committee members decided that it was imperative to present the scope of their work to the Temple College board of trustees. They would describe the forthcoming activities they would be engaging the college community in, not for approval, but for another, more pragmatic reason. She explained,

> When we knew we were going to jump into this, my committee had the absolute instinct that if we did not know before we began that we'd have the backing of the administration and the board of trustees, there was no reason to start to meet and waste our time. I asked the president if I could speak to the board at the next meeting. And when I got up, I was not on the agenda. I was part of the president's report. Knowing that this issue was so important to him and that he had put us there *on his agenda*—instead of just lumping us in with everything else took my breath away.
>
> When he turned over the president's report to me and said that this was on the top of our agenda this year, we knew we had the power to do anything. It gave me goose bumps and made me a little teary-eyed—and the other members of the committee. Before I started to speak, I turned around for a minute to draw courage from them, and one of them looked over at me and mouthed the word, "Wow" and put his hand over his heart as if to reinforce how significant this was. I made my report, thinking, "This is fabulous."

Taking the whole academic year to address the issue, the Academic Integrity Task Force, led by Summers, initiated the college's membership in CAI. To determine the extent to which the climate was right for a change, they purchased the rights to use CAI-developed surveys for faculty members and students. That fall, they surveyed hundreds of students and faculty. Their results pointed to some powerful differences of opinion between faculty members and the students they served. Summers continued to lay out the evolution of their progress:

> Once we had the data tabulated, our vice president put everything in a PowerPoint presentation, and she and the committee members presented our findings in a strategic conversation that was open to everybody—students, faculty, trustees, administrators, and staff—anyone who wanted to come. We had two presentations: one that presented the data and one that asked everyone to help prepare the solutions.

We began talking about the policy as a result of the data. We wanted two different levels of policy that addressed cheating: the simple and the more complex. We wanted the faculty to have some kind of discretion because they knew the students. We wanted to identify violations of academic integrity not as disciplinary matters, but as academic matters with academic sanctions. We asked for and received the absolute student and faculty approval for the *XF* grade, which is in its infancy in a lot of places, because we wanted to distinguish between a regular *F* and a failing grade received for cheating. We want to develop a course that students can take to rehabilitate their transcript if they receive this grade, but we want it to have real merit. We don't just want to punish; we want to teach accountability for their behavior, acknowledge the wrongness of it, and purposefully set them in another direction more in line with the ethics of learning.

What was the reaction among the faculty at large? Summers acknowledged that addressing dishonesty and promoting integrity required a climate of mutual trust and respect, not just between the faculty and administration, but among faculty members themselves:

It takes a faculty and an administration who discuss all manner of things freely. It takes an atmosphere where the faculty feel completely free to discuss any kind of issue with the administration and with each other. They need absolute freedom to say, "We want to change this" and to know that the administration will say, "That's great!" or pitch in to help with what we are doing when we need it. Our CAO helped write the policy, but we had first given her the elements we wanted. The ideal situation is one in which everyone discusses integrity and there is consensus about what you're doing.

Our Faculty Council is a special environment. In our meetings, it is possible for someone to put an issue like this on the table and have someone else stand up and say, "Oh, why are we bothering?" And then everyone else feels free enough or empowered enough to say, "Because it matters. Now sit down and listen." Then everyone else—and that person who originally stood up—sits down and laughs.

They might ask if we all really believe that things can change, and if they do, they will hear their colleagues saying, "Yes. It can. It can change." This actually happened.

Other members of the Temple College faculty, staff, administration, and board of trustees are justifiably proud of the work of the Integrity Task Force. Asked to explain the impetus that began the college's work on this issue, President Marc Nigliazzo commented,

> There's always been a sensitivity here, but until our vice president of educational services began to focus people's attention on it, we were going with what we had in the previous policies and hand-books unless we had a serious issue that shed some light on it. The interest is there, the willingness of the people to come together and discuss the issue—including the board of trustees—is there.

> The board could be very happy to just say, "Well, we know we have a policy on cheating in the student handbook. We have read it and we have approved it. What else should we do unless we've got issues that are rampant on campus and that keep bubbling up to us?" I think the positive thing about us is that there is a willingness —a genuine interest—once the subject is raised, to pursue it, to learn more about it, and to try to perfect our policies and procedures in terms of addressing it well. (M. Nigliazzo, personal communication, September 17, 2005)

Nigliazzo reflected on an athletic situation he encountered several years ago when he was new as president. The incident became exemplary of the climate of integrity that existed at the college:

> Well, the incident came up because we were about 40% through the baseball season in the spring when the athletic director, Danny Scott, came to me and said, "Dr. Nigliazzo, I have discovered that we have a couple of students taking more developmental

hours than NJCAA permits them to." And it was purely accidental. It had occurred during registration when Danny was out because of a family emergency, and this situation fell through the cracks.

When he came back in and began to go through records as he does religiously every semester, he said, "Uh-oh. It is illegal for kids to take that many developmental hours and count it as eligible." So, in essence, we had one or maybe two students who were ineligible for the teams that they participated in. I asked, "What does that mean, Danny?" and he said that we would have to forfeit. Well, I asked, "How many games is that?" and he said that it could be as many as 8 or 10 ball games, and 6 or 8 of them may have been conference games that we had won.

I said, "Danny, you know, we messed up and I don't think there's anything we can do. How are you and I ever going to look each other in the face and talk about integrity if we just knowingly let this go?" So, we turned ourselves in to NJCAA and reported what had happened. Even though it probably never would have been discovered by anybody, we would have known. If we would have done nothing, neither of us could have lived with that.

Summary of Actions Taken
Within a year, members of the Academic Integrity Task Force had accomplished the goals they had set for themselves—and for the college—and had done so in an extraordinary collaboration of effort that included faculty, students, administrators, and members of the college's board of trustees. Their specific accomplishments included the following:

- The formation of a faculty-led task force, representative of six academic divisions, student athletics, and invited members of the advising staff
- Membership in CAI and the initiation of a campuswide integrity audit, a survey of students and faculty designed to illuminate their beliefs about academic dishonesty
- Organization of two strategic conversations that invite students, faculty, administrators, and trustees to hear the complete findings, discuss possible action plans, and set priorities for the next steps

- Development of a revised academic integrity policy, which includes the adoption of an *XF* grade (designed to distinguish failure resulting from violation of the academic integrity policy) and the proposed development of an integrity curriculum designed to rehabilitate *XF* recipients and to give them a chance to expunge their academic record (Temple College, 2005)
- Integration of integrity activities into new students' orientation; division-based, part-time faculty orientations (coordinated by task force members); and ongoing professional development for faculty and staff members
- Revision of the college's mission statement to purposefully reference the college's obligation to graduate students who value integrity

Recommendations

The terrorist attacks of September 11, 2001, permanently changed the social, economic, legal, and spiritual fabric of the United States. We are intimately familiar with tragedy, irrevocably scarred by horror, wary of the world around us, and less convinced of our own security. One barometer of our uneasiness is the number of Web sites devoted to the tragedy of 9/11. A cursory search I conducted on a Web browser produced—in less than .19 seconds—precisely 114 million Web sites referencing three words: *World Trade Center*.

Oddly enough, a second search on the same browser—using three words: free term papers—yielded an astonishing 176 million Web sites in less than .05 seconds. The plague of academic dishonesty is diabolical but, in the larger scope of things, is nowhere near the evil of terrorism. However unprecedented 9/11 was in its sheer life-altering power and media fallout, it is sobering to discover a topic about which information is even more prolific or more readily available. If nothing else, it is alarming—if not perverse—evidence that the problem of academic dishonesty is an enemy to take seriously.

The four community colleges whose stories are told in this chapter are typical of the 2,000-some community colleges spread across the United States. They each reflect the dedication to the mission of teaching and learning that is the community college's legacy; they mirror the energy, compassion, forward thinking, and innovative spirit so common to many 2-year colleges. Whereas the precise number of the nation's community colleges actively engaged in the struggle against academic dishonesty is unknown, if those four institutions are any indicator of propensity toward action, we may consider the battle half won in preserving the integrity of the learning we so cherish. Of course, those four colleges may be quite atypical, because we cannot yet know how many community colleges have recognized the potential danger that academic dishonesty presents.

Some may be relying on what has seemed to work in the past and hoping that it will continue to work in the future. Some may be faced with more imminent or obvious concerns. And still others may lack the necessary climate, wherewithal, or motivation to address such a treacherous, ethereal, and persistent enemy. But for those who are ready to take formative steps toward action, knowing the first steps of others may be a helpful resource. The following nine recommendations offer advice that may prove helpful to those who take up the cause in the days, months, years, and generations to come:

- Balance the message.
- Be proactive.
- Include everyone.
- Expect resistance or cynicism, but do not yield to it.
- Nurture a comprehensive climate of integrity.
- Be an objective evaluator of organizational strengths and weaknesses.
- Learn from the lessons of others.
- Do not neglect the honest students.
- Don't just sit there: Do something.

Balance the Message

Although unethical practices may be known by more than one name (i.e., cheating or academic dishonesty), many of the nation's community colleges have well-established policies to contend with the issue in the learning environment. What is less certain is how many colleges do anything to focus their students' attention on the importance of integrity. It is imperative to address academic dishonesty; this entire book is a testament to that urgent need. As important as the punishments are that we impose when students fall short of our expectations, promoting the behaviors we want from students is equally important. As shown by the powerful example of Bill Taylor of Oakton Community College and the Oakton faculty, students more readily respond to discussions of ethics when they are made aware of the faculty's integrity obligation to them.

Be Proactive

In this chapter, each story from each college reflects the action of one person —eventually acting in concert with many—who was unwilling to allow the issue of academic dishonesty to go unaddressed. Although they each have a variety of motivations for their actions, they have one thing in common: They were proactive. When they began, they may have lacked the necessary resources presumed to be critical to transform an institution, but an odd and unpredictable thing happened: They changed it anyway—and in some profound ways. Happily, in the final analysis, the change occurred not because of the money or the positional power they might have held: It occurred because they were passionate about promoting integrity and they possessed the vision to see something better.

Include Everyone

Community colleges are microcosms of social order. Whereas many have purposefully questioned the effectiveness of rigidly separated faculty groups from other rigidly separated staff or administrative groups, many others remain traditionally structured. As a result, the issues that are designated as "faculty issues" seldom find opportunities for examination in a broader context and fail to generate the support they might have otherwise engendered in a more open environment. Those who were interviewed spoke eloquently about conversations among instructors (both part- and full-time), students (nontraditional and traditional), staff members, and administrators at all levels. Many included the surrounding community members in their discussions. The lesson learned is that cross-pollination of effort is a good thing, resulting in (a) improved understanding, (b) eventual buy-in, and (c) renewed enthusiasm—all of which have both strengthened and quickened the ability of the entire organization to respond well to an otherwise daunting enemy.

Expect Resistance or Cynicism, But Do Not Yield to It

People familiar with the precepts of political influence and leadership may recall the adage that change of any kind is difficult. Change within higher education is especially so. But, as previously noted, change—especially revolutionary change—rarely results from a majority opinion. Usually, change results from a small number of people who refuse to be intimidated and who have the ability to vanquish (or at least outlast) resistance and to bring others along. Those who described their activities to promote integrity or address dishonesty often spoke of the support they received, but they also acknowledged the presence of the "loyal opposition," whose support they had a right to expect but did not receive. Their determination—along with the results of their persistence—stands as testimony to the value of rising above cynicism or confrontation.

Nurture a Comprehensive Climate of Integrity

Too many of us assume that the battle against academic dishonesty is fought in the classroom. Nothing could be further from the truth. Where academic dishonesty occurs is only symptomatic of the issue—geography, in other words. The fight is an organizational battlefront and is as at home in the boardroom as it is in the classroom. Academia must begin to see it that way. As academicians, we model integrity for our students in the way we interact with them, prepare to engage them, and even address and punish acts of dishonesty that occur. But if we choose to respond only to dishonesty, we address only half of the problem. We teach students what is wrong, but we fail to provide a critical ethical context.

In the long run, not only are we trying to effect honesty among students, but also we are (or we should be) in the business of training purposefully ethical citizens of the world. To do anything less is to shortchange the debt we owe our respective constituencies, especially the students we are bound to serve. In other words, our own integrity is reflected in the way in which we approach the issue. We owe students—and ourselves—more than a perfunctory punitive response. We owe them evidence of ethics—in our mission statements, marketing materials, admissions applications, degree plans, articulation agreements, syllabi, Web sites, curricular agendas, college policies, honor codes, student leadership activities, and campus culture. Individually and organizationally, we must model the integrity we seek.

Be an Objective Evaluator of Organizational Strengths and Weaknesses

When academic dishonesty occurs on a campus, one inevitable truth surpasses all others: "no policy: no punishment." This pithy phase sums up the importance of predicting and preparing for cheating. Community colleges that are ready to confront the inevitable occurrence are better prepared to take the critical next steps to promote integrity. However, those who have policies in place should not stop there; more can always be done. For example,

- Review the current academic dishonesty policy for its usefulness. Was it written so long ago that no one remembers what it was intended to accomplish? Is there a lack of support among members of the faculty and student services staff for the present version? Do members of the faculty find it necessary to create their own (unofficial) responses to incidents of academic dishonesty? If any answers are "yes," it is time to discuss, revise, and adopt a policy that reflects the level of support requisite to be truly purposeful.

• Look for existing loopholes in the system. Many colleges have exemplary policies designed to address academic dishonesty, but have they looked beyond the policies for the ways in which offenders might escape compliance? I have pointed out the existence of academic clemency policies, which could (based on the parameters of their respective policies) allow students to appeal for removal of previously awarded failing grades. Grades of F received for acts of dishonesty disappear as soon as the appeal is granted. Speaking from experience, I wrote:

> What if, we asked, a student cheated, was awarded an *F* for the class, and then—perhaps years and administrations later—applied for academic clemency? No committee, no dean, would know that the *F* meant anything more than the student's inability to meet the expected level of learning for the class. We all had to admit that, under those circumstances, all *F*'s looked alike; there was no systemic way to differentiate a failing grade for cheating from a failing grade for, well, failing. Given that, chances were good that the punishment, while justifiable, would not be permanent. (Clos, 2002, pp. 1–2)

Also, consider the other systemic breaches that may be counterproductive to college integrity initiatives. For example, if an integrity policy does exist, is there a way to prevent an accused (but not yet adjudicated) student offender from dropping the course in which the act of dishonesty was committed? If not, those who are caught and confronted may be outside the reach of the punishments that would have otherwise been effected.

Learn From the Lessons of Others

Too many of us struggling with the issue of academic dishonesty do so in isolation. The bad news is that no organization is immune to the difficulties presented by dishonesty, and community colleges are no exception. The good news is that community colleges are addressing the issue of academic dishonesty and promoting the importance of integrity and their experiences—triumphs and losses. They serve to make our own organizational progress more expedient.

Consider the significant effect of the community colleges highlighted within this chapter, each having responded intuitively to the need to confront academic dishonesty and to promote academic integrity. Collectively, their accomplishments include, but are not limited to, the following:

- Membership in CAI
- Formation of academic integrity committees designed to recommend policy solutions
- Development of an Ethics Awareness Week incorporating instructional and student services functions and involving students, faculty and staff members, and administrators
- Distribution of academic integrity brochures designed to help both full- and part-time faculty members
- Initiation of a campus-based poster campaign
- Revision of course syllabi to include an academic integrity statement
- Formation of a partnership between business and industry to support academic integrity among technical students
- Revision of outdated policies, including the recommendation and eventual adoption of the *XF* grade and a remedial integrity course to assist in rehabilitating offenders
- Revision of the college mission statement to include the importance of integrity
- Initiation of campus-based strategic conversations to give students, faculty and staff members, and administrators an opportunity to discuss the results of "integrity audits" for their campus
- Development of faculty-initiated statements in support of academic integrity, and letters from faculty members to students stressing the importance of academic integrity
- Incorporation of academic integrity activities into student activities including freshman orientation, fall festivals, and spring flings

Do Not Neglect the Honest Student

Perhaps yet another ironic twist inherent to the analysis of academic dishonesty is that so little, if any, of our attention—both in the classroom and in pursuit of research—has been focused on discovering and identifying the attitudes, beliefs, and behaviors that underlie and perpetuate academic integrity. We have formulated complicated behavioral explanations for dishonest behavior—some reinforced by anecdote and personal experience—but we have very little idea what keeps an honest student honest, even when such behavior is obviously an exception to the norm.

There are reasons, no doubt, for the situation. Cheating is dastardly and must be stopped; most of us—even those whose research has been chronicled early in the evolution of this issue—agree on a sense of urgency and defensive action as we seek to protect the institution and the integrity of its mission. But perhaps it is also true that somewhere during the past 40 years, we have missed the forest for the trees. We are not saying that our efforts—individually and collectively—have been in vain. We can point with some authority to the reasons some students cite for cheating; they self-report, for example, levels of laziness, pressure, and cynicism that are difficult to conceptualize or relate to—even for the baby boomer's generation. Worse, they subscribe to an unpredictable sort of lunatic relativism that allows them to easily abandon or retrieve values that were once thought of as permanent. For some of them, there are other priorities.

It is all about competition. Rack up the high score, take home more points than all of the other players—as if college and learning could be reduced to a euphemistic two-dimensional parallel universe inside a digital game. Set your values aside and win. There is enough room for only so many, and whatever does not help you win only slows you down. The name of this game is familiar: The one with the most stuff wins. But with that game, another problem surfaces. The philosophical premise that provides the foundation for our capitalist structure is based on equity. When that equity fails, the system we now take for granted will suffer the consequence of dishonesty.

In this kind of scenario, it is seldom the righteous who inherit the grade, although that is where most academic efforts are focused. Because of a relatively traditional perspective of education, grades have always been the central focus rather than how the grades were earned. Perhaps it is too difficult to imagine having to dissect into two parts what used to be inseverable: education and integrity.

Disproportionately few researchers have raised that question. For a relatively brief period of time, the research focused on any number of individual variables including age, gender, grade point average, internal and external locus of control, social class, and religious affiliation. Most of those variables have failed to yield productive results, but more is the pity that in our attempt to grease the squeaky wheel, we neglect what may be a significant corner of the research.

Don't Just Sit There: Do Something

When confronted with seemingly insurmountable obstacles, many of us resign ourselves to defeat before we begin. Many good reasons exist for doing just that when the issue is one as persistent and indefatigable as academic dishonesty. We are confronted with many other pressing issues that call for our attention, and a day has only so many hours. But academic integrity flourishes only when we are willing to stand and defend it. The community college legacy is that we are inclined to be action-oriented even in the face of seemingly insurmountable odds. What other institution of higher education accepts virtually 100% of those who apply and exerts all of its organizational energy to make good on the promise of the open door? What other institution of higher education devotes itself to everyone with equal devotion, regardless of the academic, cultural, or social differences? Do any of us believe that the greatness of our colleges is a limited commodity, which can stretch only so far as practicable? As both a product of and practitioner in the community college, I assert that our limitations and motivations are the only relative commodity. The rest is inspiration.

References

Aaron, R. M. (1992, Winter). Student academic dishonesty: Are collegiate institutions addressing the issue? *NASPA Journal, 29*(2), 107–113. (ERIC # EJ442669)

Aaron, R. M., & Georgia, R. T. (1994). Administrator perceptions of student academic dishonesty in collegiate institutions. *NASPA Journal, 31*(2), 83–91. (ERIC # EJ477087)

Alfred, R., Shults, C., & Seybert, J. (2007). *Core indicators of effectiveness for community colleges* (3rd ed.). Washington, DC: Community College Press.

Allen, J. L. (2000, December 3). Oakton professor battles notion that cheating is just study tool. *Chicago Tribune.*

Alschuler, A. S., & Blimling, G. S. (1995). Curbing epidemic cheating through systemic change. *College Teaching, 43*(4), 123–125. (ERIC # EJ518207)

Antion, D. L., & Michael, W. B. (1983). Short-term predictive validity of demographic, affective, personal, and cognitive variables in relation to two criterion measures of cheating behaviors. *Educational and Psychological Measurement, 43*(2), 467–482. (ERIC # EJ287627)

Baird, J. S. (1980). Current trends in college cheating. *Psychology in the Schools, 17,* 512–522.

Baldwin, D. C., Jr., Daugherty, S. R., Rowley, B. D., & Schwartz, M. R. (1996). Cheating in medical school: A survey of second year students at 31 schools. *Academic Medicine, 71,* 267–273.

Barnett, D. C., & Dalton, J. C. (1981). Why college students cheat. *Journal of College Student Personnel, 22*(6), 545–551.

Batista, E. (2000, August 18). New toys for cheating students. *Wired News.*

Biddulph, C. (2004, September 17). Cheating the electronic way [Letter to the editor]. *The Chronicle of Higher Education, 51*(4), p. A47.

Bowers, W. J. (1964). *Student dishonesty and its control in college.* New York: Columbia University, Bureau of Applied Social Research.

Bricault, D. (1998). *Legal aspects of academic dishonesty: Policies, perceptions, and realities.* Retrieved January 2, 2002, from http:campus.northpark.edu/esl/dishnst.html

Burke, J. L. (1997). *Faculty perceptions of and attitudes toward academic dishonesty at a two-year college.* Unpublished dissertation, University of Georgia, Athens. (ERIC # ED431486)

Burnett, D. D., Rudolph, L., & Clifford, K. O. (Eds.). (1998). *Academic integrity matters.* Washington, DC: National Association of Student Personnel Administrators.

Burningham, J. (2004, September 17). Cheating the electronic way [Letter to the editor]. *The Chronicle of Higher Education, 51*(4), p. A47.

Bushweller, K. (1999). Generation of cheaters. *American School Board Journal, 186*(4), 24–30.

Callahan, D. (2004). *The cheating culture: Why more Americans are doing wrong to get ahead.* Orlando, FL: Harcourt.

Carnegie Council on Policy Studies in Higher Education. (1979). *Fair practices in higher education: Rights and responsibilities of students and their colleges in a period of intensified competition for enrollment.* San Francisco: Jossey-Bass.

Carnegie Foundation for the Advancement of Teaching. (1990). *Campus life: In search of community.* Princeton, NJ: Author.

Carter, S. L. (1996). *Integrity.* New York: HarperCollins.

Center for Academic Integrity. (1999, October). *The fundamental values of academic integrity.* Retrieved September 28, 2007, from www.academicin tegrity.org/fundamental_values_project/pdf/FVProject.pdf

Center for Academic Integrity. (2007). *Assessment guide.* Retrieved September 28, 2007, from www.academicintegrity.org/assessment_guide/index.php

Cizek, G. J. (2003). Detecting and preventing classroom cheating: Promoting integrity in assessment. Thousand Oaks, CA: Corwin.

Clarke-Pearson, M. (2001, November 27). Download, steal, copy: Cheating at the university. *Daily Pennsylvanian.*

Clos, K. L. (2002, November 8). When academic dishonesty happens on your campus. *Innovation Abstracts, 24*(26).

Dalton, J. C. (Ed.). (1985). *Promoting values development in college students.* Washington, DC: National Association of Student Personnel Administrators.

Dalton, J. C. (1998). Creating a campus climate for academic integrity. In D. D. Burnett, L. Rudolph, & K. O. Clifford (Eds.), *Academic integrity matters* (pp. 1–11). Washington, DC: National Association of Student Personnel Administrators.

Davis, S. F. (1993, March). *Cheating in college is for a career: Academic dishonesty in the 1990s.* Paper presented at the meeting of the Southeastern Psychological Association, Atlanta, GA. (ERIC # ED358382)

Davis, S. F., Grover, C. A., Becker, A. H., & McGregor, L. N. (1992). Academic dishonesty: Prevalence, determinants, techniques, and punishments. *Teaching of Psychology, 19*(1), 16–20.

De Russy, C. (2003, September 19). Professional ethics begin on the college campus. *The Chronicle of Higher Education, 50*(4), p. B20.

Dickerson, D. (2007). Facilitated plagiarism: The saga of term-paper mills and the failure of legislation and litigation to control them. *Villanova Law Review, 52*(Rev. 21).

Dodd, T. M. (2007). *Honor code 101: An introduction to the elements of traditional honor codes, modified honor codes, and academic integrity policies.* Retrieved September 28, 2007, from www.academicintegrity.org/educational_ resources/honor_code_101.php

Dohrmann, G. (2005, March 14). The dark side. *Sports Illustrated.*

Drake, C. A. (1941). Why students cheat. *Journal of Higher Education, 12,* 418–420.

Drinan, P. (1999). Loyalty, learning, and academic integrity. *Liberal Education, 85*(1), 28–33.

Fain, M., & Bates, P. (2005, January 27). *Cheating 101: Paper mills and you* [Seminar description]. Retrieved August 28, 2007, from www.coastal.edu/library/presentations/papermil.html

Fass, R. A. (1986). By honor bound: Encouraging academic integrity. *Educational Record, 67*(4), 32–36.

Finkel, E. (2005, February 28). Sticky fingers on the information superhighway. *Community College Week,* pp. 7–8.

Gehring, D., Nuss, E. M., & Pavela, G. (1986). *Issues and perspectives on academic integrity.* Washington, DC: National Association of Student Personnel Administrators.

Gehring, D., & Pavela, G. (1994). *Issues and perspectives on academic integrity* (2nd ed.), Washington, DC: National Association of Student Personnel Administrators.

Genesee Community College. (2006). *Student rights and responsibility handbook.* Retrieved September 28, 2007, from www.genesee.edu/students/Students_Rights_Handbook.pdf

Gerdeman, R. D. (2000, July). Academic dishonesty and the community college. ERIC Clearinghouse for Community Colleges. (ERIC # EDO-JC-00-07)

Goldsen, R. K., Rosenberg, M., William, R., Jr., & Suchman, E. (1960). *What college students think.* Princeton, NJ: Van Nostrand.

Goldsmith, H. (1998). The impact of technology on academic integrity. In D. D. Burnett, L. Rudolph, & K. O. Clifford (Eds.), *Academic Integrity Matters* (pp. 135–141). Washington, DC: National Association of Student Personnel Administrators.

Groark, M., Oblinger, D., & Choa, M. (2001, September/October). Term paper mills, anti-plagiarism tools, and academic integrity. *Educause*. Retrieved September 28, 2007, from www.educause.edu/ir/library/pdf/erm0153.pdf

Hetherington, E. M., & Feldman, S. E. (1964). College cheating as a function of subject and situational variables. *Journal of Educational Psychology, 55*, 212–218.

Hollinger, R. C., & Lanza-Kaduce, L. (1996). Academic dishonesty and the perceived effectiveness of countermeasures: An empirical survey of cheating at a major public university. *NASPA Journal, 33*, 292–306.

Houston, J. P. (1976). The assessment and prevention of answer copying on undergraduate multiple-choice examinations. *Research in Higher Education, 5*, 301–311.

Howe, N., & Strauss, W. (2000). *Millennials rising: The next great generation.* New York: Vintage Books.

Howe, N., & Strauss, W. (2003). *Millennials go to college.* Washington, DC: American Association of Collegiate Registrars and Admissions Officers.

Huber, J. (2004). A, B, or cheat. *APTE News, 25*(2), 23–25.

Jendrek, M. P. (1989, September). Faculty reactions to academic dishonesty. *Journal of College Student Development, 30*, 401–406. (ERIC # EJ406563)

Jendrek, M. P. (1992, May). Students' reactions to academic dishonesty. *Journal of College Student Development, 33*, 260–273. (ERIC # EJ446968)

Johnston, D. K. (1996). Cheating: Limits of individual integrity. *Journal of Moral Education, 25*, 159–171.

Josephson Institute of Ethics. (2002). *Survey documents decade of moral deterioration: Kids today are more likely to cheat, steal, and lie than kids 10 years ago.* Available from www.josephsoninstitute.org

Josephson Institute of Ethics. (2004). *2004 Josephson Institute report card on the ethics of American youth. Part 1: Integrity.* Retrieved September 6, 2007, from www.josephsoninstitute.org/Survey2004/2004reportcard_pressrelease.htm

Kaplin, W. A., & Lee, B. A. (1995). *The law of higher education.* San Francisco: Jossey-Bass.

Keith-Spiegel, P., Tabachnick, B., Whitley, B. E., Jr., & Washburn, J. (1998). Why do professors ignore cheating? Opinions of a national sample of psychology instructors. *Ethics and Behavior, 8,* 215–227.

Keith-Spiegel, P., Wittig, A., Perkins, D., Balogh, D., & Whitley, B. E., Jr. (1993). *The ethics of teaching: A casebook.* Muncie, IN: Ball State University Press.

Kerkvliet, J., & Sigmund, C. L. (1999). Can we control cheating in the classroom? *Journal of Economic Education, 30*(4), 331–343.

Kibler, W. L. (1993). Academic dishonesty: A student development dilemma. *NASPA Journal, 30,* 252–267.

Kibler, W. L. (1998). The academic dishonesty of college students: The prevalence of the problem and effective educational prevention programs. In D. D. Burnett, L. Rudolph, & K. O. Clifford (Eds.), *Academic integrity matters* (pp. 23–37). Washington, DC: National Association of Student Personnel Administrators.

Kibler, W. L., Nuss, E. M., Peterson, B. G., & Pavela, G. (1988). *Academic integrity and student development: Legal issues, policy perspectives.* Asheville, NC: College Administration Publications. (ERIC # ED367277)

Kroft, S. (2005, September 4). *The echo boomers.* CBS News. Retrieved September 28, 2007, from www.cbsnews.com/stories/2004/10/01/60min utes/printable646890.shtml

Lumsden, D. B., & Arvidson, C. (2001, Winter). Academic integrity among community college students: Findings of a preliminary investigation. *The Catalyst,* pp. 1–6. Available from http://findarticles.com/p/articles/mi_ qa4011/is_200101/ai_n8931754

Maramark, S., & Maline, M. B. (1993). *Academic dishonesty among college students: Issues in education.* Washington, DC: Office of Educational Research and Improvement.

McCabe, D. L. (1992). The influence of situational ethics on cheating among college students. *Social Inquiry, 63,* 365–374.

McCabe, D. L. (1993). Faculty responses to academic dishonesty: The influence of student honor codes. *Research in Higher Education, 34,* 647–658.

McCabe, D. L. (1999). Academic dishonesty among high school students. *Adolescence, 34*(136), 681–687.

McCabe, D. L. (2005, June). *CAI research* [Web site page]. Available from www.academicintegrity.org/cai_research/index.php

McCabe, D. L., & Klebe Treviño, L. (1993). Academic dishonesty: Honor codes and other contextual influences. *Journal of Higher Education, 64*(5), 522–538.

McCabe, D. L., & Klebe Treviño, L. (1996). What we know about cheating in college: Longitudinal trends and recent developments. *Change, 26*(1), 28–33.

McCabe, D. L., & Klebe Treviño, L. (1997). Individual and contextual influences on academic dishonesty: A multi-campus investigation. *Research in Higher Education, 38,* 379–396.

McCabe, D., & Klebe Treviño, L. (2002, January/February). Honesty and honor codes. *Academe.* Retrieved September 28, 2007, from www.aaup.org/publications/Academe/2002/02JF/02jfmcc.htm

McCabe, D. L., Klebe Treviño, L., & Butterfield, K. D. (1996). The influence of collegiate and corporate codes of conduct on ethics-related behavior in the workplace. *Business Ethics Quarterly, 6,* 461–476.

McCabe, D. L., Klebe Treviño, L., & Butterfield, K. D. (1999). Academic integrity in honor code and non-honor code environments: A qualitative investigation. *Journal of Higher Education, 70,* 211–234.

McCabe, D. L., Klebe Treviño, L., & Butterfield, K. D. (2001). Cheating in academic institutions: A decade of research. *Ethics and Behavior, 11*(3), 219–232.

McCabe, D. L., & Pavela, G. (1997). Ten principles of academic integrity. *Journal of College and University Law, 24,* 117–118.

Moeck, P. (1999). *Medical assisting program student resource manual.* Denton, TX: RonJon.

Moeck, P. (2002). Academic dishonesty: Cheating among community college students. *Community College Journal of Research and Practice, 26,* 479–491.

Moffatt, M. (1990). *Undergraduate cheating.* Unpublished research report, Rutgers University, New Brunswick, NJ. (ERIC # ED334921)

Morgan, B., Korschgen, A., & Gardner, J. (1996, August). *Students' and professors' views on the ethics of faculty behavior.* Paper presented at the meeting of the American Psychologyical Association, Toronto, Canada. (ERIC # ED409752)

Niels, G. J. (1996). *Is the honor code a solution to the cheating epidemic?* Unpublished research paper, Columbia University, New York, NY. (ERIC # ED423191)

Nuss, E. M. (1984). Academic integrity: Comparing student and faculty attitudes. *Improving College and University Teaching, 32*(3), 140–144.

O'Neil, T. D. (2003, November 8). *Technology and academic integrity: Cheating goes cyber.* Retrieved September 28, 2007, from http://isedj.org/isecon/2003/3513/ISECON.2003.ONeil.pdf

Oakton Community College. (n.d.). *Promoting integrity in academic life and beyond.* Retrieved August 28, 2007, from http://servercc.oakton.edu/~pboisver/NewFaculty/FacAcadIntegr.htm

Oakton Community College. (2001). *Our vision, mission, and values.* Retrieved August 28, 2007, from www.oakton.edu/visitor/mission.htm

Pavela, G. (1978, February 9). Cheating on campus. Who's really to blame? *The Chronicle of Higher Education, 21*(22), 64.

Pavela, G. (1988). The law and academic integrity. In W. L. Kibler, E. M. Nuss, B. C. Peterson, & G. Pavela (Eds.), *Academic integrity and student development: Legal issues, policy perspectives.* Asheville, NC: College Administration Publications. (ERIC #ED367277)

Peterson, L. (1988). Teaching academic integrity: Opportunities in bibliographic instruction. *Research Strategies, 6*(4), 168–176.

Plagiarism is rampant, a survey finds. (1990, April 1). *New York Times*, p. 36.

Rafetto, W. G. (1985, October/November). The cheat. *Community and Junior College Journal, 56*(2), 26–27.

Read, B. (2004, July 16). Some professors go beyond honor codes to stop misuse of electronic devices. *The Chronicle of Higher Education, 50*(45), p. A27.

Renard, L. (2000, December/January). Cut and paste 101: Plagiarism and the net. *Educational Leadership*, 38–42.

Rimmington, G. (2004, September 17). Cheating the electronic way [Letter to the editor]. *The Chronicle of Higher Education, 51*(4), p. A47.

Roberts, P., Anderson, J., & Yanish, P. (1997, October). *Academic misconduct: Where do we start?* Paper presented at the meeting of the Northern Rocky Mountain Educational Research Association, Jackson, WY. (ERIC # ED415781)

Rocklin, T. (1996). *Downloadable term papers: What's a prof. to do?* Retrieved August 28, 2007, from www.uiowa.edu/~centeach/resources/ideas/term-paper-download.html

Rookstool, J. (2007). *Fostering civility on campus.* Washington, DC: Community College Press.

Roueche, J., Johnson, L., & Roueche, S. (1997). *Embracing the tiger: The effectiveness debate and the community college.* Washington, DC: American Association of Community Colleges.

Sandeen, A. (1985). The legacy of values education in college student personnel work. In J. C. Dalton (Ed.), *Promoting values development in college students* (pp. 1–5). Washington, DC: National Association of Student Personnel Administrators.

Schemo, D. J. (2001, May 10). U. of Virginia hit by scandal over cheating. *New York Times.* Retrieved September 28, 2007, from www.csie.ntu.edu.tw/~lyuu/virginia.html

Schneider, E. H. (1999, January 22). Why professors don't do more to stop students who cheat. *The Chronicle of Higher Education,* pp. A8–A10.

Sierles, F., Hendricks, I., & Circle, S. (1980). Cheating in medical school. *Journal of Medical Education, 55,* 124–125.

Sims, R. L. (1993). The relationship between academic dishonesty and unethical business practices. *Journal of Education for Business, 68,* 207–211.

Singhal, A. C. (1982). Factors in students' dishonesty. *Psychological Reports, 51,* 775–780.

Singhal, A. C., & Johnson, P. (1983). How to halt student dishonesty. *College Student Journal, 17*(1), 13–19.

Smyth, M. L., & Davis, J. R. (2003). An examination of student cheating in the two-year college. *Community College Review, 31,* 17–33.

Spiegel, J. (1999). *The time has come to tackle academic cheating* [Brochure]. Princeton, NJ: Educational Testing Service.

Stern, E. B., & Havlicek, L. (1986). Academic misconduct: Results of faculty and undergraduate student surveys. *Journal of Allied Health, 15*(2), 129–142. (ERIC # EJ335490)

Strauss, W., & Howe, N. (1991). *Generations: The history of America's future, 1584–2069.* New York: Morrow.

Strauss, W., & Howe, N. (1997). *The fourth turning: An American prophecy.* New York: Broadway Books.

Tabachnick, B., Keith-Spiegel, P., & Pope, K. (1991). Ethics of teaching: Beliefs and behaviors of psychologists as educators. *American Psychologist, 46,* 506–515.

Taylor, W. M. (n.d.). *Academic integrity: A letter to my students.* Retrieved August 28, 2007, from http://servercc.oakton.edu/~pboisver/NewFaculty/LetterTaylor.htm

Temple College. (2005). *Academic integrity policy.* Retrieved August 28, 2007, from www.templejc.edu/academic/AcadInteg/AcadIntegrity.htm

Templeton, J. M., & Schwartz, A .J. (1999). *College and character* [Introduction]. In John Templeton Foundation (Ed.), *The Templeton guide: Colleges that encourage character development* (pp. 1–3). West Conshohocken, PA: Templeton Foundation Press. Retrieved September 28, 2007, from www.collegeandcharacter.org/guide/introduction.html

Vaughan, G. B. (1992). *Dilemmas of leadership: Decision making in the community college.* San Francisco: Jossey Bass. (ERIC # ED348103)

Weiss, K. R. (2000, February 15). Focus on ethics can curb cheating, colleges find. *The Los Angeles Times.*

Whitley, B. E., Jr. (1998). Factors associated with cheating among college students: A review. *Research in Higher Education, 39*(3), 235–274. (ERIC # EJ567552)

Whitley, B. E., Jr., & Keith-Spiegel, P. (2002). *Academic dishonesty: An educator's guide.* Mahwah, NJ: Erlbaum.

Wilson, R. (1998, July 31). Professor says UCLA retaliated against him for reporting cheating incident. *The Chronicle of Higher Education,* p. A9.

Wingspread Group on Higher Education. (1993). *An American imperative: Higher expectations for higher education.* Racine, WI: Johnson Foundation, Inc.

Wolfe, D. T., & Hermanson, D. R. (2005, June 19). The fraud diamond: Considering the four elements of fraud. *CPA Journal.*

Wotring, K. E. (2007). Cheating in the community college: Generational differences among students and implications for faculty. *Inquiry, 12*(1), 5–13. Retrieved September 28, 2007, from www.vccaedu.org/inquiry /inquiry-spring-2007/i-12-Wotring.html

Young, J. R. (1997, August 15). Distributors of term papers over the Internet are warned. *The Chronicle of Higher Education.*

Appendix A:
Bill Taylor's Letter to Students About Academic Integrity

Academic Integrity: A Letter to My Students

Here at the beginning of the semester I want to say something to you about academic integrity. (The *American Heritage Dictionary* defines integrity as the "steadfast adherence to a strict moral or ethical code.") I'm deeply convinced that integrity is an essential part of any true educational experience, integrity on my part as a faculty member and integrity on your part as a student.

To take an easy example, would you want to be operated on by a doctor who cheated his way through medical school? Or would you feel comfortable on a bridge designed by an engineer who cheated her way through engineering school? Would you trust your tax return to an accountant who copied his exam answers from his neighbor?

Those are easy examples, but what difference does it make if you as a student or I as a faculty member violate the principles of academic integrity in a political science course, especially if it's not in your major?

For me, the answer is that integrity is important in this course precisely because integrity is important in all areas of life. If we don't have integrity in the small things, if we find it possible to justify plagiarism or cheating or shoddy work in things that don't seem important, how will we resist doing the same in areas that really do matter: in areas where money might be at stake, or the possibility of advancement, or our esteem in the eyes of others?

Personal integrity is not a quality we're born to naturally. It's a quality of character we need to nurture, and this learning process requires practice in both meanings of that word (as in practice the piano and practice a profession). We can be a person of integrity only if we practice it every day.

What does that (integrity) involve for each of us in this course? Let's find out by going through each stage in the course. As you'll see, academic integrity basically requires the same things of you as a student as it requires of me as a teacher.

I. Preparation for Class

What Academic Integrity Requires of Me in This Area

With regard to coming prepared for class, the principles of academic integrity require that I come having done the things necessary to make the class a worthwhile educational experience for you. This preparation requires that I

- Reread the text (even when I've written it myself).
- Clarify information I might not be clear about.
- Prepare the class with an eye toward what is current today (that is, not simply rely on past notes).
- Plan the session so that the presentation will make it worth your while to be there.

What Academic Integrity Requires of You in This Area

With regard to your coming prepared for class, the principles of academic integrity suggest that you have a responsibility to yourself, to me, and to the other students to do the things necessary to put yourself in a position to make fruitful contributions to class discussion. This preparation will require you to

- Read the text before coming to class.
- Clarify anything you're unsure of (including looking up words you don't understand).
- Formulate questions you might have so you can ask them in class.
- Think about the issues raised in the directed reading guide.

II. In Class

What Academic Integrity Requires of Me in This Area

With regard to class sessions, the principles of academic integrity require that I take you seriously and treat you with respect. This approach requires that I

- Show up for all class sessions unless I'm simply unable to do so.
- Come to class on time and not leave early.
- Not waste class time, but use it well to fulfill the objectives of the course.
- Do my best to answer your questions.
- Honestly acknowledge when I don't have an answer or don't know something, and then go out and get an answer by the next class.
- Both encourage you, and give you an equal opportunity, to participate in class discussions.
- Contain you if your enthusiasm for participating in the discussions makes it difficult for others to participate.

- Assume that you are prepared for class and that I won't embarrass you if I call on you, even if your hand isn't up.
- Respect the views you express and not make fun of you or of them.
- Not allow others to ridicule you or your ideas, or you to do the same to them.
- Make clear when I am expressing an opinion, and not impose on you my views on controversial issues.

What Academic Integrity Requires of You in This Area

With regard to class sessions, the principles of academic integrity require you to take both me and your fellow students seriously and to treat us with respect. This approach requires that you

- Show up for all class sessions unless you are simply unable to do so.
- Come to class on time and not leave early.
- Make good use of class time by being engaged in what's going on.
- Ask questions about anything you don't understand, and not just for your own sake but because other students might not realize that they also don't understand.
- Participate in the class discussions so as to contribute your thinking to the shared effort to develop understanding and insight (remember that even something that's clearly wrong can contribute to the discussion by stimulating an idea in another student that he or she might not otherwise have had).
- Monitor your own participation so as to allow for and encourage the participation of others.
- Respect the other students by not making fun of them or their ideas,and by not holding side-conversations that distract them (and me) from the class discussion.

III. With Regard to Exams

What Academic Integrity Requires of Me in This Area

With regard to exams, the principles of academic integrity require that I

- Do my best during class time to prepare you for the exams.
- Be available during office hours or at arranged times to work with you individually to help you get ready for the exams.

- Develop exam questions that will be a meaningful test not only of the course content. but also of your ability to express and defend intelligent judgments about that content.
- Carefully monitor the exam so that honest students will not be disadvantaged by other students who might choose to cheat if given the opportunity.
- Give due and careful consideration to your answers when evaluating them and assigning a grade.

What Academic Integrity Requires of You in This Area

With regard to exams, the principles of academic integrity require that you

- Come to class having done your best to prepare for the exam, including seeking my help if you need it.
- Make full use of the time available to write the best answers you can.
- Accept your limitations and not try to get around them by using cheat sheets, copying, or seeking help from another student.
- Do not give help to other students, or make it easy for them to copy off you.

IV. With Regard to Written Assignments

What Academic Integrity Requires of Me in This Area

With regard to written assignments, the principles of academic integrity require that I

- Devise meaningful assignments that grow out of and further the work done in the classroom.
- Provide you with a clear description of that assignment so that you know what is expected of you and what I'll be looking for when I grade it.
- Give due and careful consideration to your paper when evaluating it and assigning a grade.
- Confront you if I suspect that you have plagiarized or in other ways not handed in work that is entirely your own.

What Academic Integrity Requires of You in This Area

With regard to written assignments, the principles of academic integrity require that you

- Start your research and writing early enough to ensure that you have the time you need to do your best work.
- Hand in a paper that you yourself have done specifically for this course and have not borrowed from someone else or recycled from an earlier course.
- Do not be satisfied with a paper that is less than your best work.
- Seek only appropriate help from others (such as proofreading, or discussing your ideas with someone else to gain clarity in your thinking).
- Give full and proper credit to your sources.

Let me expand on this last point, because it applies to both you and me. By its very nature, education and the accumulation of knowledge form a shared enterprise. None of us has the time, let alone the background knowledge required, to learn everything on our own. Virtually everything we know has come to us because someone else has taken the time to think about something, research it, and then share what he or she has learned with us in a class lecture or, more likely, in an article or book. This acquisition of knowledge is every bit as true for me as a teacher as it is for you as students. I'd have very little to teach if all I could talk about is what I've learned solely on my own.

In a class lecture, it would be too disruptive if I stopped to cite all of my sources, but I know, and you need to know, that I am sharing with you the things I've learned from hundreds of different authors. What I contribute is the way I bring their ideas together into a coherent whole so that it makes sense to you.

If this process is true for me, how much more so is it for you. I have many more years of education and reading behind me than you do. I don't expect you to do original research. Instead, I expect you to read about the research of others and to bring together their ideas in such a way that makes sense to you and will make sense to me. Therefore, it's essential for you to cite your sources in any research paper you write. The academic reasons for doing so are to give credit to those who have done the original research and written the article or book, and to allow me to look at them if I needed to find out if you have properly understood what the author was trying to say.

But at a practical level, citing your sources is a way to show that you've done the assignment. If your paper contains no citations, the implication is that you have done a piece of original research, but that wasn't the assignment. Citations (along with the bibliography) show that you have consulted a variety of resources as the assignment required. They're also an acknowledgment of your indebtedness to those authors. So don't feel you need to hide the fact that you're drawing from one of your sources. That's what it's all about.

V. With Regard to Your Final Grade

What Academic Integrity Requires of Me in This Area
With regard to your final grade, the principles of academic integrity require that I carefully weigh all of your grades during the course, as well as the other factors that affect the final grade as spelled out in the syllabus, before I assign a final grade.

What Academic Integrity Requires of You in This Area
With regard to your final grade, the principles of academic integrity require that, if you feel I've made a mistake in computing that grade, you have a responsibility to come to me as soon as possible prepared to show why you think I've made a mistake.

VI. Failures to Live up to Our Responsibilities
In all of the areas listed above, I will do my best to live up to my responsibilities. If you feel I've failed to do so, you have every right to call me on it. If you do, I have a responsibility to give you respectful consideration. If you feel that I do not do these things, you have the right (and I would say the responsibility) to bring this matter to the attention of my dean.

At the same time, I have a right to expect that you will live up to your responsibilities. If I get a sense that you're not doing so, I consider it a matter of my academic integrity that I call you on it. Indeed, in certain circumstances (such as cheating or plagiarism), I may be required to charge you with a violation of the College's Code of Academic Conduct. The college is every bit as committed to academic integrity as I am.

You should familiarize yourself with that Code. You can find it in the student handbook; it's also summarized on page 39 in the College Catalog. Be sure to notice that there's a procedure that's designed to protect your rights. But that procedure might also result in one or another sanction being imposed on you if you're found guilty of violating the Code of Academic Integrity.

That brings me to the most difficult question with regard to academic integrity; what if you become aware of a fellow classmate who is not living up to the principles of academic integrity, but you sense that I'm not aware of it? What should you do? I'll give you the answer, but I'll acknowledge up front that it's a hard one. Nevertheless, I would hope that you would at least grapple with it if you are ever confronted with the situation. The answer is that you should say something to that student, and if worse comes to worse, you should tell me. But why? Academic integrity, as with so much in life, involves a system of interconnected rights and responsibilities that reflect our mutual dependence upon one another. The success of our individual efforts in this course, as with so much in life, depends on all of us conscientiously exercising our rights and living up to our responsibilities. And the failure of any of us—even just one of us—to do what is required will diminish, however slightly, the opportunity for the rest to achieve their goals. That is why it's essential for all of us in this class to practice academic integrity, in both senses of the word practice. Our practice today will lay a solid foundation for practice tomorrow and the day after that and the day after that. Through daily practice, integrity will come to be woven throughout the fabric of our lives and thus through at least a part of the fabric of society.

William M. Taylor
Oakton Community College
Des Plaines, IL

Note. The author based this letter on ideas contained in the first draft of "The Fundamental Values of Academic Integrity," a document that was developed by, and is available from, the Center for Academic Integrity. Adapted from Taylor (n.d.) by permission.

Appendix B:
Oakton Community College Statement on Academic Integrity

Promoting Integrity in Academic Life and Beyond

We faculty members at Oakton Community College, sharing a commitment to academic integrity, acknowledge that one of our professional responsibilities is to model the kind of integrity we wish our students to develop. By letting them know that the norms of academic integrity apply every bit as much to us as they do to them, and then living up to those standards, we can bear witness to the values that motivate us as professionals. In so doing, we believe we will foster the growth of integrity in the lives of our students.

To that end, we pledge to conduct our professional lives in accordance with the standards of behavior spelled out below in the list of strategies for promoting academic integrity, choosing from that list those practices that best fit our teaching style and the circumstances under which we teach. We also pledge to talk with our students about our commitment to academic integrity, letting them know what they can expect from us and what we expect from them.

Strategies for Promoting Academic Integrity

I. When Preparing a Course

With regard to preparing a course, a faculty member can promote academic integrity by

- giving careful consideration to the syllabus to make sure it is updated to reflect the latest scholarship and the best available texts;
- spelling out clearly in the syllabus the nature of the work required of the students, the criteria for grading, and any expectations he or she might have of the them;
- respecting copyrights, trademarks, and patents (on software, for example); and
- planning to talk about what integrity requires of the students as each new task occurs (exams, written or lab assignments, group work, oral presentations, etc.).

II. At the Beginning of the Semester

At the beginning of the semester, a faculty member can promote academic integrity by

- providing the students with a syllabus that clearly spells out course requirements, teacher expectations, and the grading process and
- discussing why he or she is committed to academic integrity and why integrity is important for the discipline, perhaps including examples of how professionals in the discipline have violated those principles, and the consequences of those violations.

III. When Preparing for Class

With regard to preparing for class, a faculty member can promote academic integrity by doing the things necessary to make the class a worthwhile educational experience for the students. This approach can be done by

- staying up to date on recent scholarship and trends in the discipline, as well as the current issues;
- giving credit to his or her sources;
- rereading the assigned text materials, and/or working out problems ahead of time, in preparation for class;
- clarifying information he or she might not be clear about;
- recognizing that some subjects may be uncomfortable for some students and trying to find ways to deal with those issues in a direct, constructive manner;
- preparing the class with an eye toward what is current today (that is, not simply relying on past notes); and
- creating opportunities for intellectual growth rather than devoting class time to a recitation of facts or restating what the students can learn for themselves by reading the text.

IV. In Class

With regard to class sessions, a faculty member can promote academic integrity by taking her or his students seriously and treating them with respect. This approach can be done by

- showing up for all class sessions, unless he or she is simply unable to do so;
- coming to class on time, and for the most part, not ending the class early or keeping the class late;

- not wasting class time, but using it well to fulfill the objectives of the course;
- fostering and expecting mutual respect among the students and creating a safe environment in the classroom;
- talking about and modeling for students the file-sharing and downloading protocols, as well as showing respect for software licensing rights;
- doing his or her best to answer the students' questions, or arranging to do so outside class;
- being especially careful when a student asks what might be considered a "dumb" question, or one that was just answered;
- honestly acknowledging when he or she doesn't have an answer or doesn't know something, and then going out and getting an answer by the next class;
- making clear when he or she is expressing an opinion, and not imposing on the students her or his views on controversial issues;
- respecting the views the students express and not making fun of the students or their views;
- treating all students the same and not playing favorites in applying the policies spelled out in the syllabus;
- both encouraging the students and giving each of them an equal opportunity to participate in class discussions;
- containing those students whose enthusiasm for participating in the discussion makes it difficult for others to participate;
- discussing discipline-related ethical dilemmas that the teacher has faced and how he or she dealt with them;
- engaging in an ongoing process of self-evaluation of the effectiveness of teaching methods and of whether students are learning from those methods;
- not allowing students to ridicule other students or their ideas;
- not talking with students about other students or faculty members;
- adequately preparing students to do the class assignment or activity;
- providing equal opportunity and treatment for all students, such as not modifying syllabus requirements unless willing to do so for all students;
- encouraging the students to ask her or him and not their classmates for help with assignments and laboratories;
- working to identify students who look as though they may not have the study skills and/or study habits necessary to succeed without cheating, and either working with them to help them develop those skills and habits, or taking them to the Learning Center where they can get help; and

- knowing what his or her students are capable of doing by watching them work in laboratory situations.

V. With Regard to Student Contact Outside Class

With regard to being available to students outside class, a faculty member can promote academic integrity by

- being available during office hours or at arranged times to work with students on an individual basis; and
- returning calls and e-mails in a timely fashion.

VI. With Regard to Exams

With regard to exams, a faculty member can promote academic integrity by

- doing his or her best during class time, and through appropriate and meaningful out-of-class assignments, to prepare the students for the exams;
- developing exam questions that will be a meaningful test not only of the course content, but also of the student's ability to express and defend intelligent judgments about that content;
- making clear what constitutes a violation of academic integrity with regard to exams;
- setting up the classroom in such a way that it reduces the chances of cheating;
- carefully monitoring all exams to ensure fairness and to ensure that honest students will not feel disadvantaged by other students who might choose to cheat if given the opportunity;
- being consistent in his or her policy regarding makeup exams;
- being aware of the fatigue factor when grading exams; and
- giving due and careful consideration to exam answers when evaluating them and assigning a grade.

VII. With Regard to Written Assignments

With regard to written assignments, a faculty member can promote academic integrity by

- devising meaningful assignments that grow out of and further the work done in the classroom;

- making clear what constitutes a violation of academic integrity with regard to written assignments (i.e., what constitutes "doing your own work");
- providing students with a clear written description of all written assignments so they know what is expected of them and what the teacher will be looking for when grading them;
- providing students with samples of well-written assignments;
- finding out if students know how to do the assignment, and, if not, teaching them how to do so;
- looking at the students' work at the various stages of a long-term assignment;
- giving due and careful consideration to the papers when evaluating them and assigning a grade;
- returning assignments in a timely fashion; and
- confronting students whom he or she suspects of having plagiarized or in other ways not handed in work that is entirely their own.

VIII. With Regard to Assigning Final Grades

With regard to assigning the grade the student earned, a faculty member can promote academic integrity by

- having, and adhering to, a clear process and set of criteria for grading spelled out in the syllabus;
- helping students know throughout the course of the semester what grade they are earning;
- carefully weighing all of the student's grades during the course, as well as the other factors that affect the final grade as spelled out in the syllabus, before assigning a final grade; and
- giving respectful consideration to students who question the grade.

IX. With Regard to Academic Integrity Violations

With regard to possible academic integrity violations on the part of students, a faculty member can promote academic integrity by

- not overlooking a possible violation, but taking the time and making the effort to determine if a violation did occur;
- not violating the confidentiality of students who bring information about academic integrity violations; and

- being familiar with and following the college's policy on dealing with academic integrity violations.

Note. Adapted from Oakton Community College (n.d.).

Index

In page references, bold type indicates tables.

A

Aaron (1992)
  context of academic dishonesty, 20–21
  promoting academic integrity, 90, 108
  research focusing on community colleges,
    35–36, 40
Aaron and Georgia (1994)
  ethical deterioration, 32–33
  promoting academic integrity, 108
  research focusing on community colleges,
    36–37
  why academic integrity matters, 52–53
academic affairs officers, 35
  See also chief academic officers
academic clemency, 130, 133, 137
academic dishonesty (in general)
  characteristics, 27–28
  context, xi–xii, 7–23, 31–32
  defining, xi, 7–8, 25–27
  persistent nature, 19–20
  prevalence, 28–29, 34–47, 48–51
  See also specific aspects and behaviors
academic environment
  comprehensive climate of integrity, 136
  faculty perceptions and attitudes, 40
  promoting academic integrity, 79
  student and faculty perspectives compared,
    66–67
  student perceptions and attitudes, 57–60
  why academic integrity matters, 51–53
  See also institutional entries; specific aspects
academic ethics. *See* ethics
Academic Integrity Assessment Guide, 106
academic integrity policies. *See* policies
  and procedures
academic integrity promotion. *See* promoting
  academic integrity
Academic Integrity Task Force (author's
  experience), 2
Academic Integrity Task Force (Temple
  College), 126, 128–129, 131, 132
accountability
  context of academic dishonesty, 10, 22
  promoting academic integrity, 84
Adams, Mary, 117

adjudication. *See* reporting and adjudication
administrators
  context of academic dishonesty, 7, 12
  faculty perceptions and attitudes, 39–41,
    54–55
  inclusive approach, 135
  North Harris Community College story, 114
  promoting academic integrity, 79–82, 86,
    88, 91, 108
  Pueblo Community College story, 121,
    123, 124
  research focusing on community colleges,
    35–37
  student perceptions and attitudes, 47, 58–59
  Temple College story, 129–132
  trust between faculty and administrators,
    39, 130–131
  See also specific roles
advisors
  as source of integrity policies, 58–59
  Temple College story, 132
advocacy beyond the campus, 101–109
age as factor
  generational differences, 10, 93–95
  research focusing on community
    colleges, 34
  research focusing on honest students, 139
  student perceptions and attitudes, 42, 47
Alschuler and Bliming (1995), 13, 20–21
answer keys, posting of, 96–97, 99
Antion and Michael (1983), 42–43
associate faculty members. *See* part-time
  faculty
Association for Student Judicial Affairs, 121
athletes, student. *See* student athletes
attitudes of faculty and students. *See* faculty
  perceptions and attitudes; student
  perceptions and attitudes
audits, integrity. *See* integrity audits

B

baby boomers, 93, 94, 139
Baird (1980), 32
Barton County Community College, context
  of academic dishonesty, 11
basketball players
  author's experience with academic
    dishonesty, 4–5
  context of academic dishonesty, 11
  See also student athletes

About the Author

Karén Clos Bleeker is vice president of educational services and chief academic officer of the Temple College District, a position she has held since 2004. An "adopted" daughter of Texas, Clos Bleeker is a graduate of John F. Kennedy High School in San Antonio. After graduating from high school, she became a community college student, attending St. Philip's College for one year before transferring to Trinity University and earning a BA in sociology. Clos Bleeker also earned an MA in adult education from the University of Incarnate Word in San Antonio, as well as a second MA from The University of Texas at San Antonio and a doctorate in educational administration from The University of Texas at Austin. During her graduate studies, she received fellowships from the American Association of University Women as well as the Roueche Fellowship, the W. K. Kellogg Fellowship, and the Sid W. Richardson Fellowship awarded by the Community College Leadership Program. Clos Bleeker's doctoral research explored transformational leader behaviors of Texas community college board members, and her research was supported and published by the Association of Community College Trustees.

Clos Bleeker has three decades of experience in higher education including full-time and associate faculty positions as well as a variety of administrative positions with both 2- and 4-year colleges and universities. Prior to her current roles at Temple College, she served as a GED/ESL program director, counselor, assistant to the chancellor, director of institutional research, and dean of learning and instruction. Among her professional contributions, Clos Bleeker initiated and coordinated a grant-funded women's nontraditional career training program as a part of the National Institute for Leadership Development, which received national recognition from the Wider Opportunities for Women Program in Washington, DC. She has also authored dozens of articles and made numerous conference presentations on a variety of topics including academic integrity, assessment of student learning and institutional effectiveness, leadership, organizational climate and communication, and student retention, motivation, and achievement. She has twice been recognized by The University of Texas at Austin Community College Leadership Program as a visiting scholar and was awarded senior fellow status by the Texas Higher Education Coordinating Board in fall

2004. Clos Bleeker was inducted into the Edgewood Independent School District Hall of Fame in San Antonio, Texas, as a distinguished alumnus.

In addition to her professional activities, Clos Bleeker has been involved in public service on a variety of boards and steering committees including the Children's Hospital Advisory Board, Scott and White Hospital in Temple, Texas; the Taylor Foundation Board (ex officio); the Barton County Advisory Committee on Minority Affairs in Great Bend, Kansas; the Educational Service Center Region 20 Literacy Board in San Antonio, Texas; the American Association of Women in Community Colleges, West Valley-Mission Chapter in Saratoga, California; and the Rotary Club of Temple.